Introduction

A note to teachers and parents...

This book has been produced and revised to meet with specific criteria:

- To produce excellent revision notes for the end of Key Stage 2 National Curriculum Tests (SATs) for levels 3–5 inclusive, and to ensure that everything in the Programme of Study for this Key Stage is covered. Great care has been taken to ensure that everything on which the pupils could be assessed has been covered in the book – and nothing more.
- To reflect the excellent scheme of work produced by QCA in association with the Standards and Effectiveness Unit of the Department for Education and Skills.
- To encourage and retain the interest of pupils at Key Stage 2. In order to do this we have tried to make the design of this new edition even more user-friendly, using **reduced line lengths, simple language, diagrams and colour** to enhance the clarity of explanations.
- To cover the material without reference to specific levels. Every page is accessible to all pupils, but obviously some will absorb and understand more than others. All pupils should be encouraged to cover as much as possible of every topic.
- To help teachers make their way through the minefield of the National Curriculum. This book provides a concise summary of the work covered throughout Years 3–6.
- To provide, in conjunction with the accompanying Worksheet Book, an ideal classroom resource for pupils at this Key Stage.

We feel sure this guide will lighten your load and lead to a significant overall improvement in your National Curriculum Key Stage 2 test results.

A note about the consultant editor...

This book was fully revised under the expert guidance of Roger Mitchell, Chair of the Association for Science Education's Primary Science Committee. Roger is also a member of the ASE Primary Science Review Editorial Board, QCA Key Stage 2 Science Test Review Group and the SCAA Monitoring the Implementation of the National Curriculum working group.

A note about the revised programme of study for national curriculum 2000...

Although this guide covers all the changes that came into effect in September 2000, we have deliberately avoided any over-elaboration of the effects of air on plant growth because of the problems associated with demonstrating this experimentally to pupils aged 11 and under.

A note to the pupil...

We're sure that you will enjoy using this book, but here are some tips to help you get the most out of it:

- Read each section carefully and then answer the questions set. Have your answers checked regularly and go back through any work you have got wrong.
- Try to get into a routine. Work through the book steadily; don't rush and don't try to do too much at once.

Good luck!

Life Processes and Living Things

Materials and their Properties

Contents

Physical Processes

Life Processes and Living Things

Living and Non-Living Things

Everything on our planet can be divided into two groups: **living things** and **non-living things**. Movement usually tells us whether something is living – but think about the examples in the question box alongside!

To be sure if an animal or plant is living or not we need to see if it shows certain **life processes**. We may sometimes need to look very carefully or for quite a long time.

1 Tick the ones you think are alive:

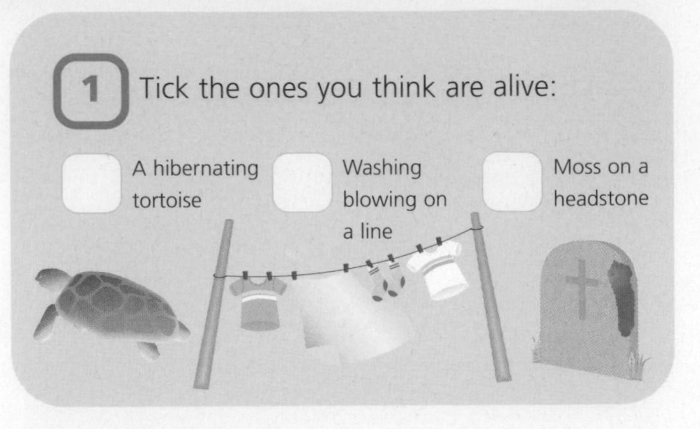

Animal Life Processes

For animals we must look for these **five** life processes:

1. **movement**
2. **growth**
3. **nutrition (feeding)**
4. **reproduction**
5. **using senses** smell, sight, taste, touch, hearing

Plant Life Processes

For plants we need to look very carefully for these **four** life processes:

1. **movement**
2. **growth**
3. **nutrition** plants make food using sunlight
4. **reproduction**

2 Tick the four things which all animals and plants do.

- [ ] Play
- [x] Sleep
- [x] Grow
- [x] Move
- [x] Reproduce
- [ ] Kill things to eat
- [ ] Hibernate
- [x] Feed

Teeth and Dental Care

Teeth are very important for breaking our food into more manageable pieces, then grinding the food up before we swallow it.

Humans have two sets of teeth. The first set appears between 3 and 6 months after birth. They are called **milk teeth**. These are gradually replaced by the **permanent teeth** which have to last us through our adult life.

We have 3 different types of teeth:

1 Incisor	2 Canine	3 Premolars and Molars
For cutting and snipping food into smaller pieces.	For piercing and tearing tough food. They're not as important for us as they are for other animals	For grinding and crushing food. They have large, flat surfaces to help them to do this.

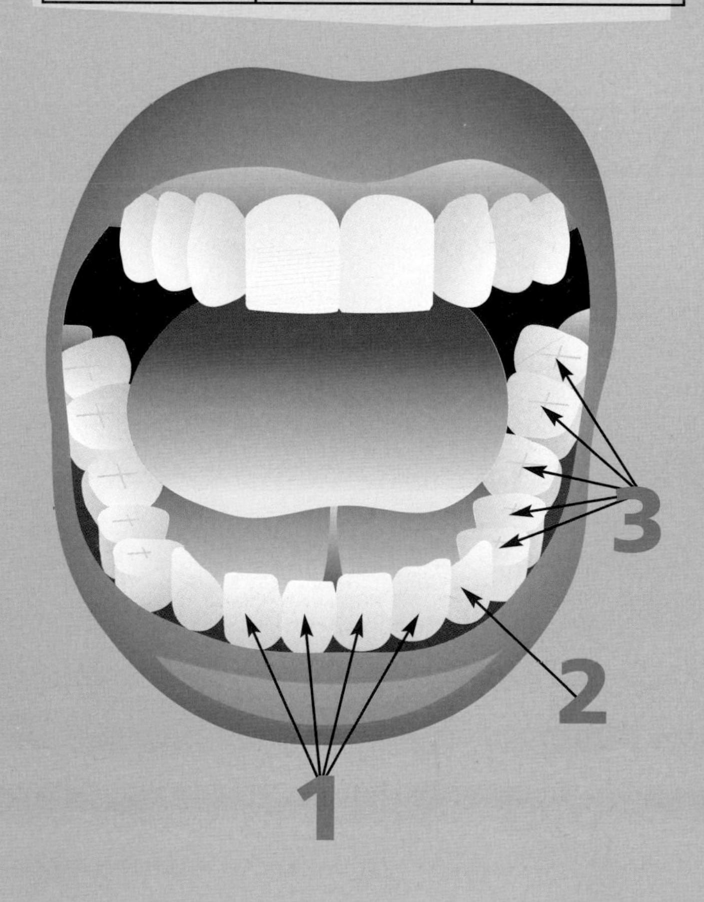

Teeth must be brushed properly at least twice a day, preferably first thing in the morning and last thing at night. This removes sugary substances which may have built up during the day, and provides a fresh, clean mouth first thing in the morning.

Brushing stops **plaque** from building up on your teeth. You can see whether you have plaque by using special tablets which colour it red. Brushing also stops sugary food being turned into **acid** which can dissolve holes (**decay**) in your teeth.

In addition to this, you must go for regular dental checks and try to eat fresh, crisp foods such as raw carrot and apple to keep your gums healthy.

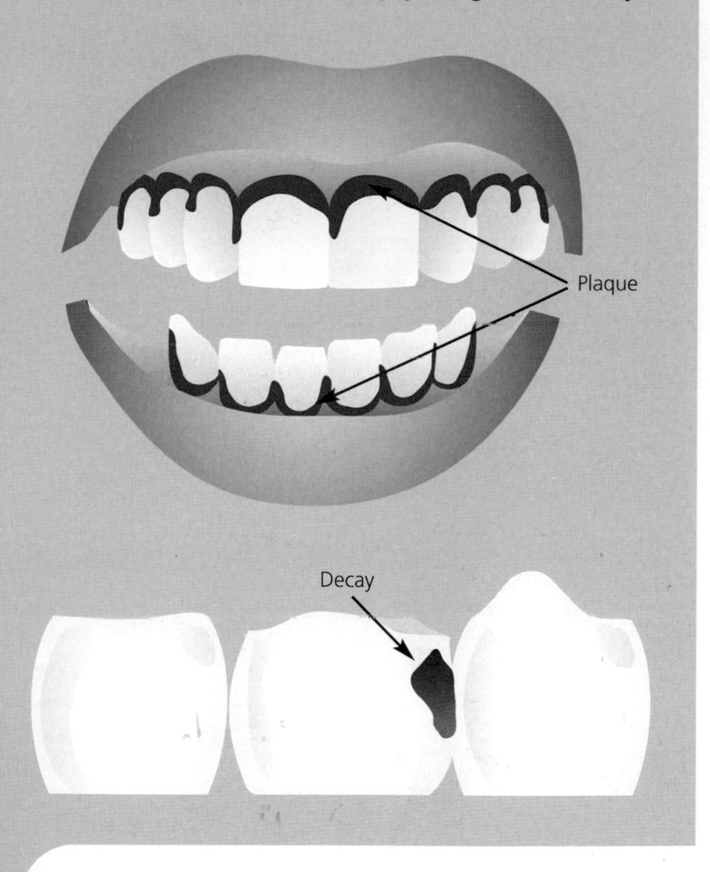

Study the different types of teeth opposite.

3. Why do you think animals like lions and tigers have large canines?
4. Why do animals like sheep have no canines at all?
5. Danny brushed his teeth before going to bed and then decided to have a sugary sweet. His mother said this was bad for his teeth. Explain why this is so.

Food Types

A healthy diet means providing yourself with the right amount of foods for **growth** and **activity**, and also trying to cut down on certain foods which may damage your teeth or cause you to become overweight.

The foods for **energy** and **activity** are either:

- **starchy foods**, such as potatoes, bread, carrots and cereals, or
- **sugary foods** such as sweets.

Fatty foods also provide a lot of energy, but too much fat should be avoided.

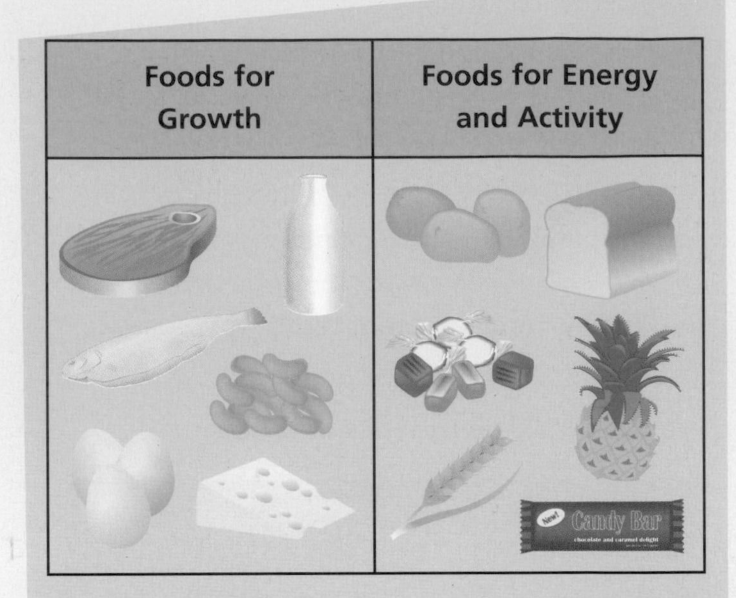

6 Sort the following food types out into food for **energy**, **growth** and **fatty foods**.

Foods you shouldn't eat too much of	What could happen if you do
Foods high in sugar	Tooth Decay
Foods high in fat	Too much of these foods may cause you to become overweight and they may eventually cause your blood vessels to block up

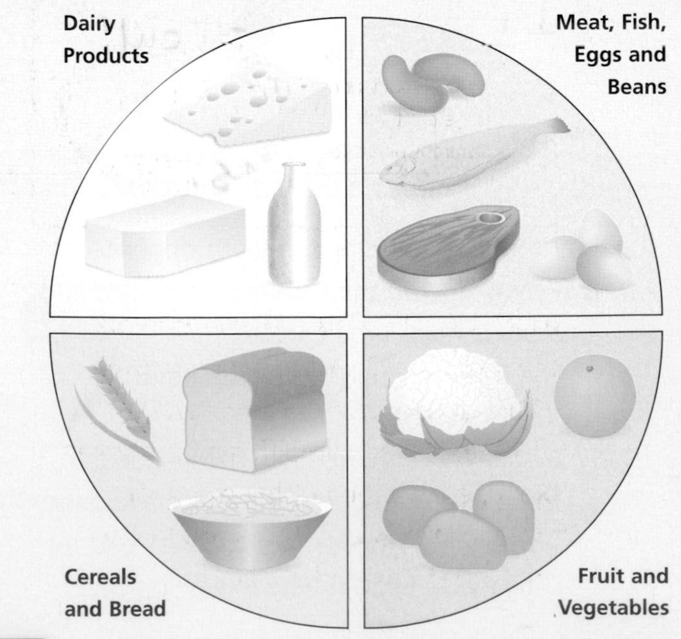

A Healthy Diet

A healthy diet should try to include one portion of food from each of the four groups every day. However, you should try to pick different foods to give you variety and also eat more of the bottom two groups (cereals and bread, and fruit and vegetables).

7 Plan a menu for a full day's healthy eating, including breakfast, lunch and dinner.

8 Describe the sort of meals that might be eaten during a day by a person on an unhealthy diet.

The Heart

The heart pumps blood through our circulatory system so that every part of the body can receive **food** and **oxygen** from the blood. The heart is made of **muscle** and beats about 70 times per minute at rest.

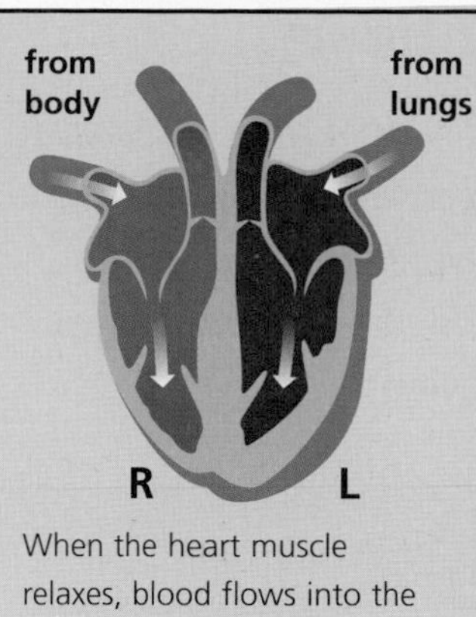

When the heart muscle relaxes, blood flows into the upper chambers of the heart through two blood vessels from the body and the lungs. From here it flows into the lower chambers.

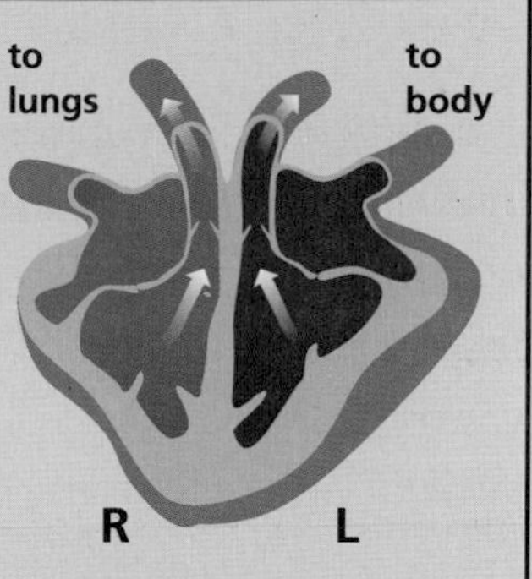

When the heart muscle contracts (squeezes), blood is forced out of the lower chambers into two blood vessels which carry blood to the body and the lungs. The blood can't flow backwards because of valves in the heart.

9 **a)** In which of the two diagrams is the blood in the heart under the least pressure?
b) In which of the two diagrams does the heart contain the least blood?

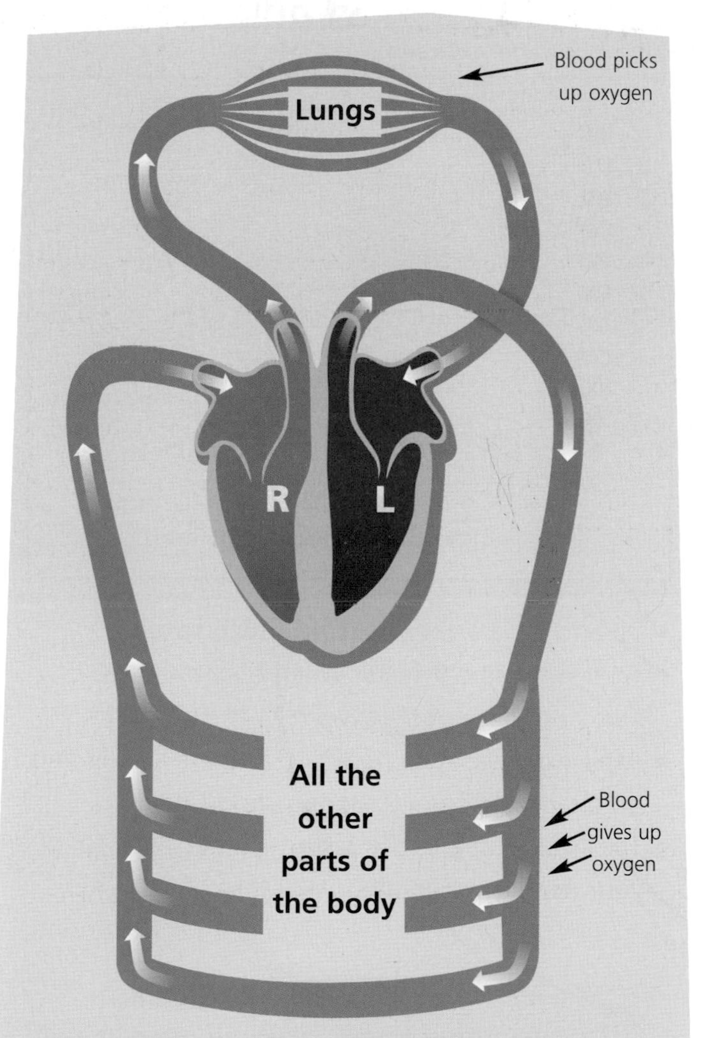

William Harvey (1578–1657) explained how blood was circulated around the body by the heart. Before he came up with this idea people thought that food was converted into blood by the liver and was then used as a fuel by the body.

The Circulation

The blood travels around the body in **blood vessels**. These blood vessels also carry blood to the lungs where they pick up **oxygen**.

In the diagram on the left-hand side of the page, blood which contains oxygen is coloured red. We can see that blood rich in oxygen travels from the lungs to the heart and is then pumped to the body, where it gives up its oxygen.

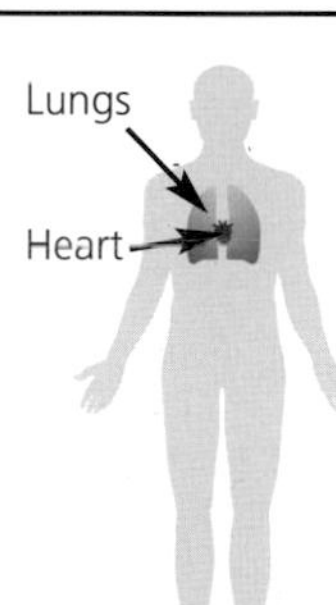

Both sides of the heart contract (squeeze) at exactly the same time. The left side pumps blood to the body and the right side pumps blood to the lungs.

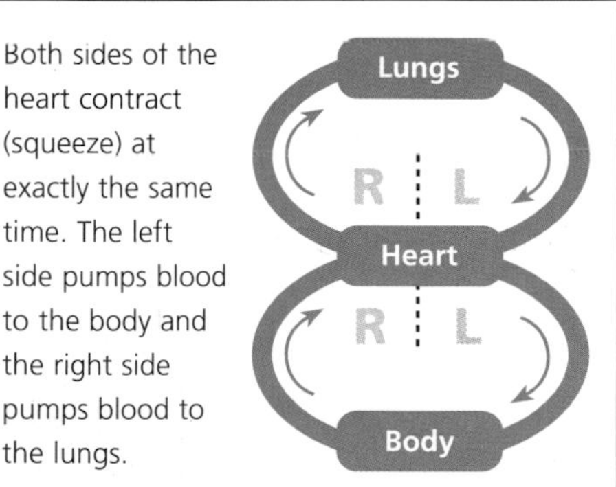

10 **a)** Which side of the heart has to do the most work? Explain your answer. (Clue: Look where the lungs are!)
b) What is the main difference between blood leaving the left-hand side of the heart and blood returning to the right-hand side of the heart?

Keeping a Healthy Heart

The heart has its own blood supply through special arteries called the **coronary arteries**. These are the arteries which get blocked when someone has a **heart attack** (a 'Coronary'). There are three ways in which your chances of having this type of problem are increased:

1. **Smoking** – The chemicals in smoke can make the walls of the blood vessels sticky.

2. **Eating Too Much Fat** – The fat can stick to the inside of the blood vessels, and gradually builds up.

3. **Not Exercising Enough** – Your blood flow will become slow because your heart muscle has become weaker. This increases the chance of a blockage.

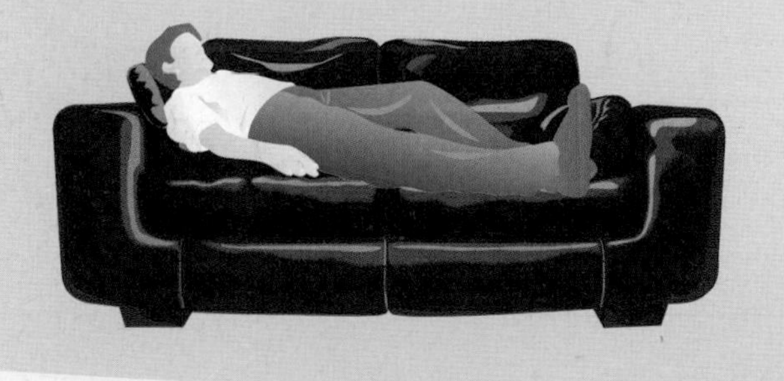

Fat Build-up in a Blood Vessel

The Effect of Exercise on Pulse Rate

Yasmin and James were investigating **heart rate** by counting each other's **pulses** for one minute, and then running round the school yard and counting them again every three minutes. The pulse is actually the flow of blood through an artery from one contraction of the heart muscle.

	James	Yasmin
Before Exercise	72	78
After Exercise	178	180
3 minutes after Exercise	142	124
6 minutes after Exercise	98	88
9 minutes after Exercise	90	78
12 minutes after Exercise	82	78
15 minutes after Exercise	72	79

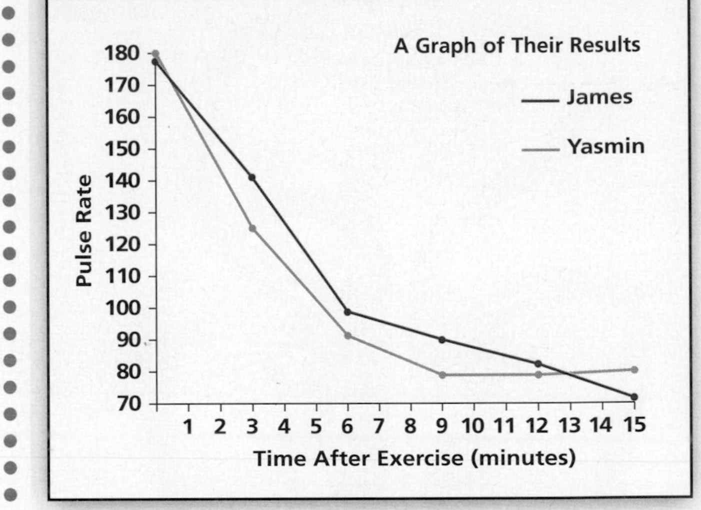

- 72 and 78 are their **resting pulse rates**.
- Their hearts beat faster when they exercise. This is to carry more oxygen to their muscles.
- After exercise, their hearts beat more slowly and gradually get back to their resting rates.
- The fitter you are, the faster you get back to your resting pulse rate.

11 Try this exercise yourself and plot your own graph. Take your pulse at your wrist or at the side of your neck (don't press too hard).

12 Design a poster for 'keep a healthy heart' week.

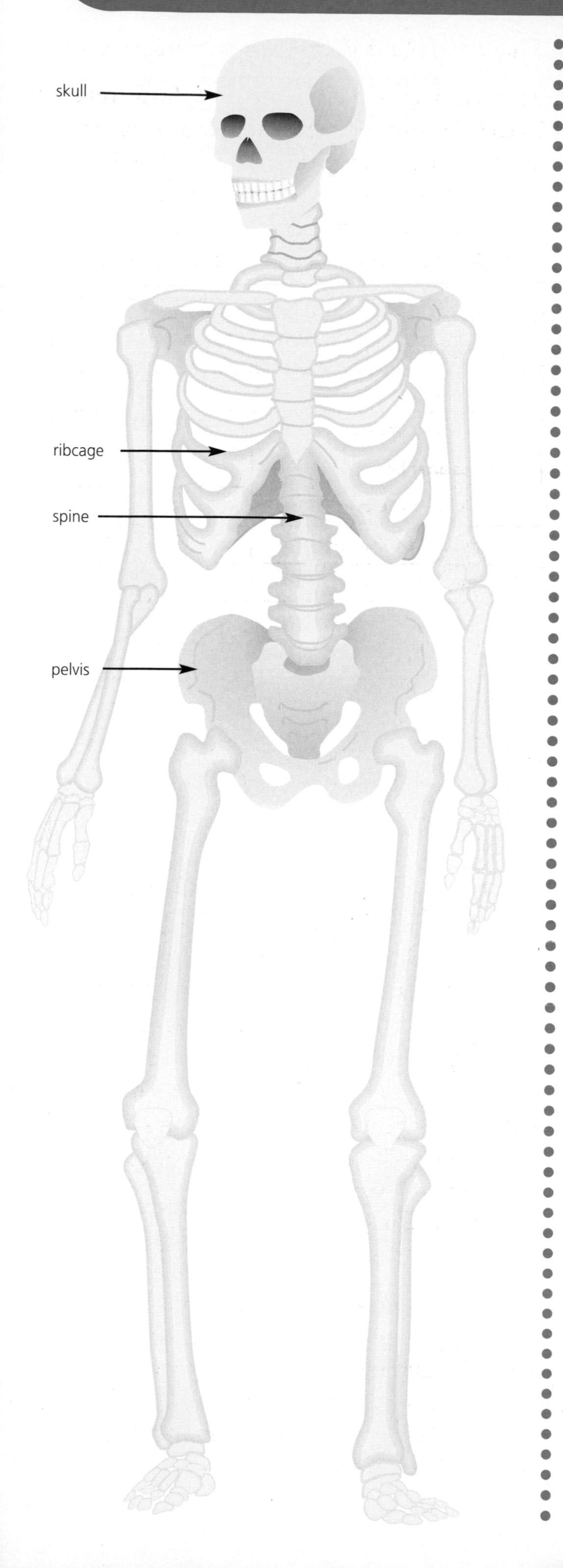

Skeleton and Movement

Humans, together with some other animals, have bony skeletons inside their bodies, which grow as they grow. The skeleton does 3 main jobs for us:

1. It **supports** all the soft bits in our bodies – without a skeleton we would be very floppy.
2. It **protects** our important organs, such as the brain, heart and lungs.
3. It helps in **movement** because muscles are attached to the bones.

13 **a)** Which organs are protected by **(i)** the skull **(ii)** the ribcage **(iii)** the pelvis?
b) Describe how you would investigate whether boys have longer arms than girls.

Muscles and Movement

Muscles can either contract (shorten) or relax. When they do either of these things along with other muscles, they usually move our bones.

In diagram 1: Muscle A has relaxed and Muscle B has contracted. So the forearm is raised.
In diagram 2: Muscle A has contracted and Muscle B has relaxed. So the forearm is lowered.

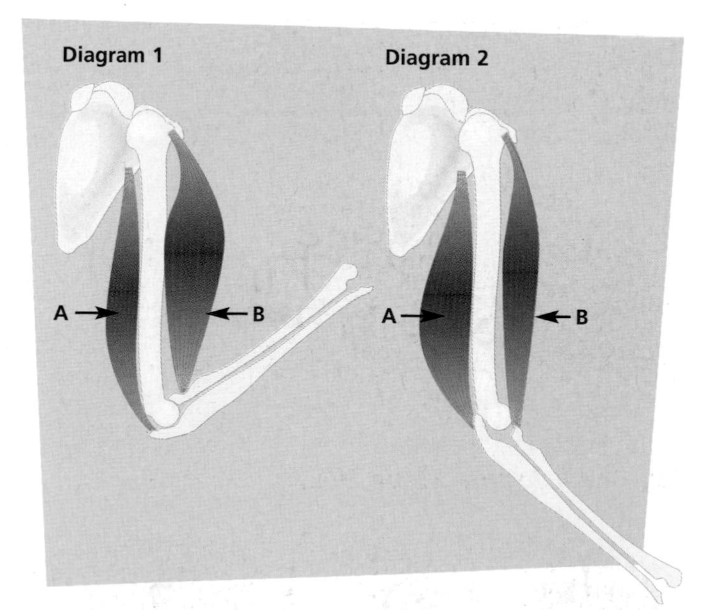

14 What would muscles A and B have to do if you wanted to hold your forearm rigid?

Life Processes and Living Things

Growth and Reproduction

The human life cycle describes the development and reproduction of humans. The stages vary from individual to individual and often occur at different times.

a) To help you remember the sequence of the life cycle below, think of a sentence, the words of which begin with the letters BGAACF.

b) Which of these stages have 9 months between them?

The Human Life Cycle

Birth
after 9 months developing inside the mother

Growth
mainly gradual but sometimes in spurts

Adolescence
changing from a child to an adult

Adulthood
emotionally and sexually grown up

Courtship
choosing a partner for reproduction

Fertilisation
occurs after sexual intercourse when a sperm meets an egg

Health

Some common substances can cause health problems:

Tobacco: Better to avoid at all costs!

- Beware! Besides actually smoking, you can also be at risk if you spend too long in smoky places or with people who smoke a lot. You will breathe in a fair amount of their smoke and all the horrible things in it. This is called **passive smoking**.
- Cigarettes contain: tar, nicotine, particles of ash, carbon monoxide.
- Smoking can cause: throat and mouth cancer, lung infections, lung cancer, bronchitis, arterial disease and heart disease

Alcohol: Best to drink in small quantities (when you're old enough!).

- Drinking too much alcohol can cause: liver damage, brain damage, poor judgement, alcohol addiction.

Other Drugs: Solvents are extremely dangerous and can cause hallucinations, personality change and damage to organs. Never, ever get involved with solvents! Any drug which is not prescribed by your doctor may cause you harm, particularly if taken in large doses.

16 Design a poster to persuade young people not to smoke.

17 Design a poster to persuade older people to drink less.

Microorganisms

Microorganisms, or **microbes** are usually too small to be seen, however, they are living organisms. You may have heard of names like bacteria, viruses, and fungi (if you haven't don't worry). Microbes fall into **two** distinct groups...

- those which have harmful effects
- those which have a useful job to perform.

Have a look at the table on the right.

18 Write a short story about a scientist who produces a drug which kills all microbes. What would happen?

☹ Harmful Microbes	☺ Useful Microbes
• Can cause illnesses such as German measles, chicken pox, colds and flu. • Can cause boils and tooth decay.	• Some microbes 'feed' on dead material and waste. This causes it to decay and release nutrients back into the soil. • Yeast is a microbe which is used to make bread rise. It is also used in wine and beer making.

Life Processes and Living Things

Effect of Light on Plant Growth

Charlotte decided to investigate how light affected plant growth. She took a tray of cress seedlings and placed it under a light-proof cardboard box. She found that after a few days the covered seedlings had grown longer but were pale yellow and spindly. When they were left in the light, they became green again after a few days.

Plants need light in order to grow well.

Effect of Water on Plant Growth

Katie decided to investigate how water affected plant growth. She took 3 trays of cress seedlings and gave the first no water, the second 10cm^3 per day, and the third 30cm^3 per day.

No water
(After 5 days) Mainly dried out and dead.

10cm^3 per day
(After 5 days) Healthy and growing.

30cm^3 per day
(After 5 days) Roots waterlogged and nearly all dead.

Plants need water to grow, but too much will kill them.

19 Describe what Charlotte, Katie and Christopher would have had to do to make sure they had performed a fair test when investigating the effect of water on plant growth.

Effect of Temperature on Plant Growth

Christopher decided to investigate how temperature affected plant growth. He took 2 trays of cress seedlings and placed one outside on the lawn in the middle of a very cold, frosty spell in January. The other one he put inside his father's greenhouse. After 5 days he measured them. The ones outside measured around 2cm, the same height they started at. The ones inside the greenhouse were also 2cm to start with, but now most of them were over 4cm!

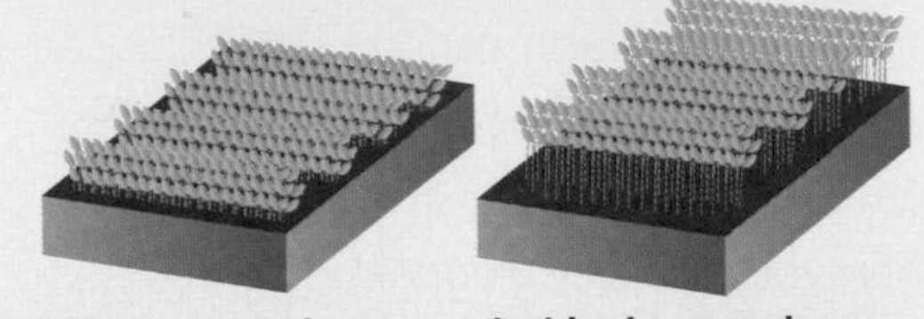

outside the greenhouse **inside the greenhouse**

Plants grow very slowly when they're very cold.

Effect of Air on Plant Growth

Charlotte, Katie and Christopher found out from their textbook that plants also need something from air in order to grow healthily. They placed a bell jar over some seedlings and removed all the air using a vacuum pump. They did this every day in case some air had managed to get inside the bell jar. After 5 days their seedlings were looking yellow and limp.

Plants need something in the air to grow properly.

Life Processes and Living Things

Flower Structure

The male parts of the flower are the **stamens**. They consist of two parts:

- The **filament** which holds...
- The **anther** which produces pollen.

The female part of the flower is the **carpel**. This is made up of three parts:

- The **stigma** which receives pollen grains.
- The **style** which is a narrow tube.
- The **ovary** which contains the egg cell inside an **ovule**.

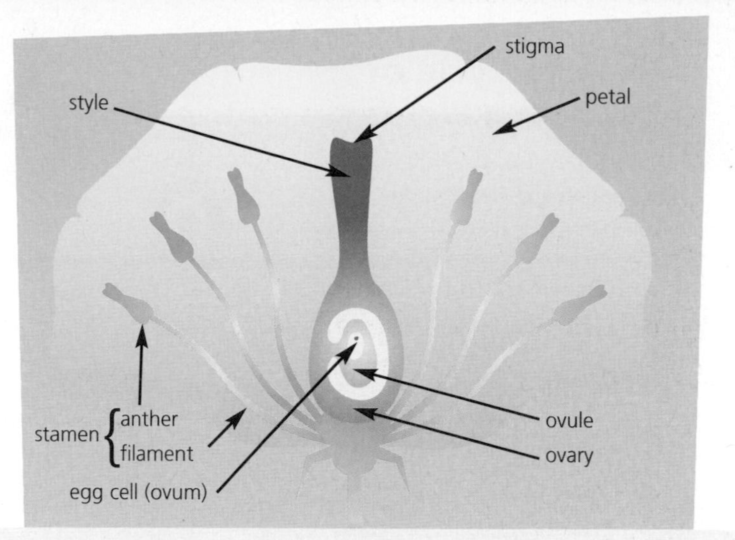

20 **a)** Which part of the flower produces pollen?
b) Is this the male or female part?
c) Which part of the flower receives pollen?
d) Is this the male or female part?

Stem and Leaves

- The leaves of green plants make new material for growth from **air** and **water** in the presence of **light**. They also make and store food for the plant.
- The light is 'captured' by the leaves.
- The water is transported from the roots through the stem to other parts of the plant.

Mia put a stick of celery in some red dye. After an hour she took it out and cut it in half. This is what she saw when she looked at the cut end.

The red dye in the water had travelled up the stem in special tubes!

21 If Mia left the stick of celery in the dye for over a day, what might happen to the leaves?

Roots

- The roots anchor the plant, and take in **water** and some **nutrients** from soil. **Plants do not take in food through their roots.**
- Different plants grow in different soil conditions and some also store food in their roots. This means roots can look very different ...

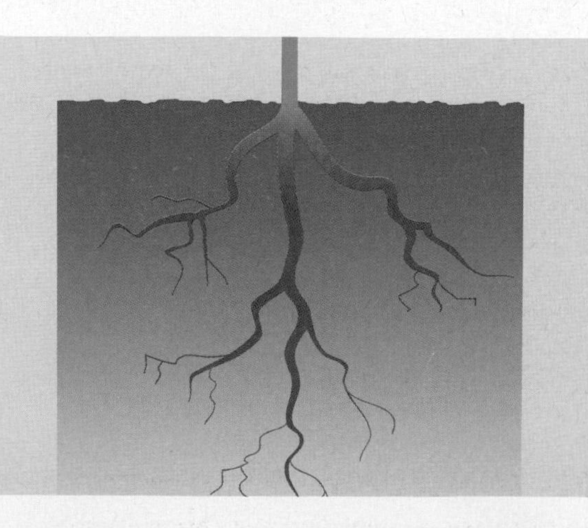

fibrous roots | carrot roots | potato roots | deep roots

22 What type of root would you expect in plants which live on very sandy soil?

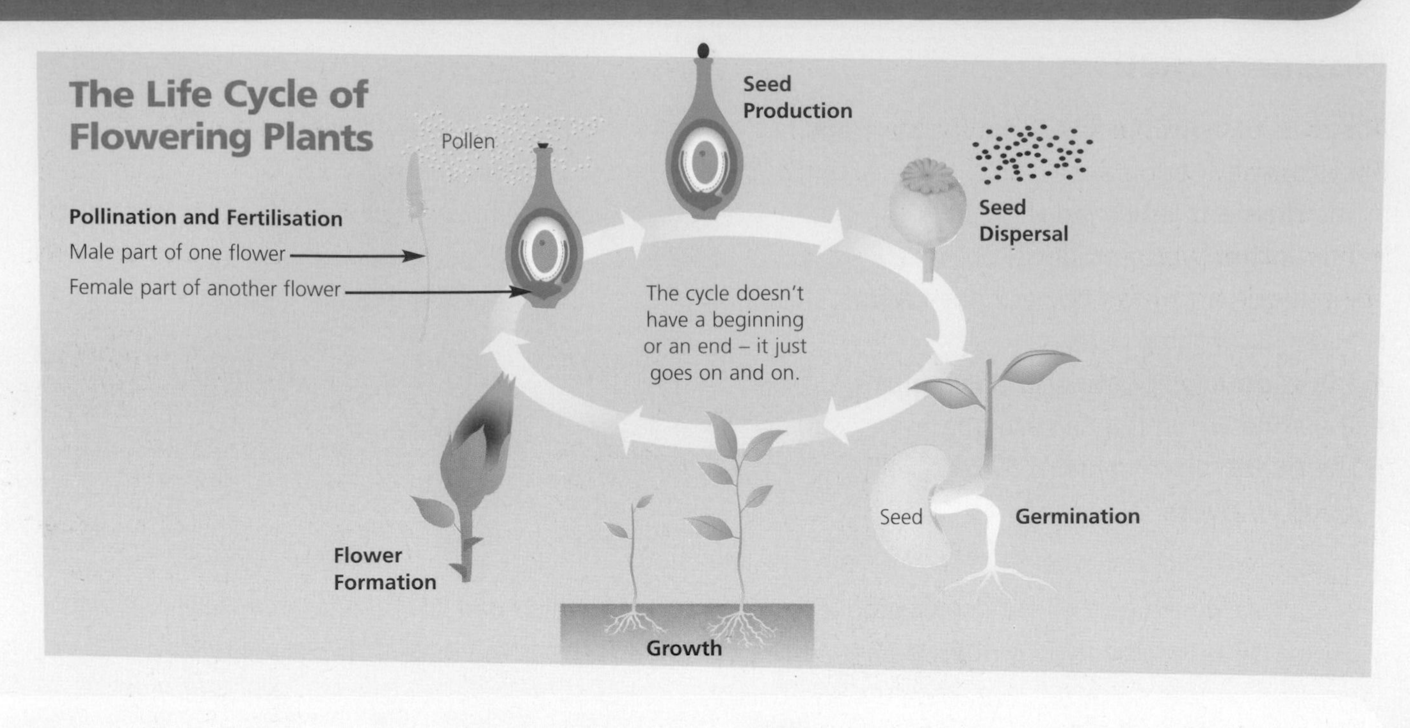

23 Which two of these stages of the cycle do you think take the least amount of time?

24 Which two stages do you think would take the longest amount of time?

Pollination

Pollination is when pollen from the anthers of one plant gets on to the stigma of another. This is usually done by the **wind** or by **insects**. Flowers have different special features depending upon whether they use wind or insects to pollinate.

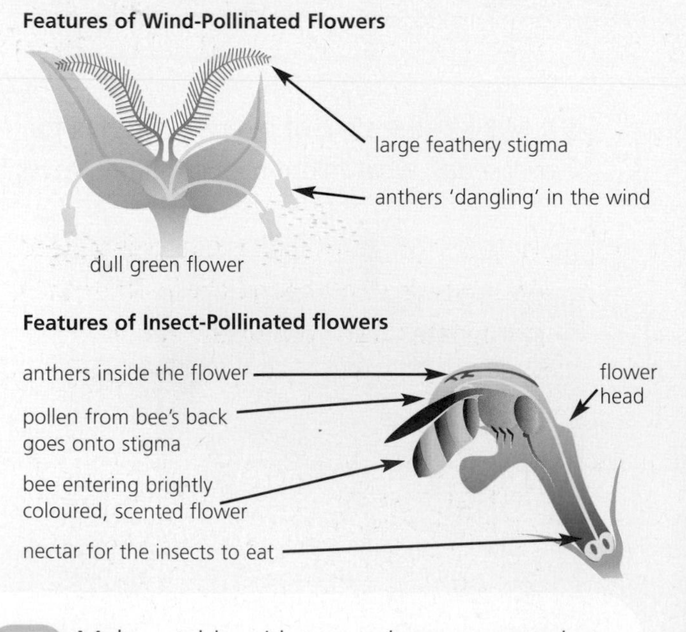

25 Make a table with two columns comparing the differences between wind and insect pollinated flowers. Concentrate on things like anthers, stigma, nectar, colour and scent.

Fertilisation

Fertilisation is the name given to the process in which a tube from the pollen grain grows down towards the ovum (egg cell) and joins up with it. This is the beginning of a new plant and leads to the next stage – **seed production**.

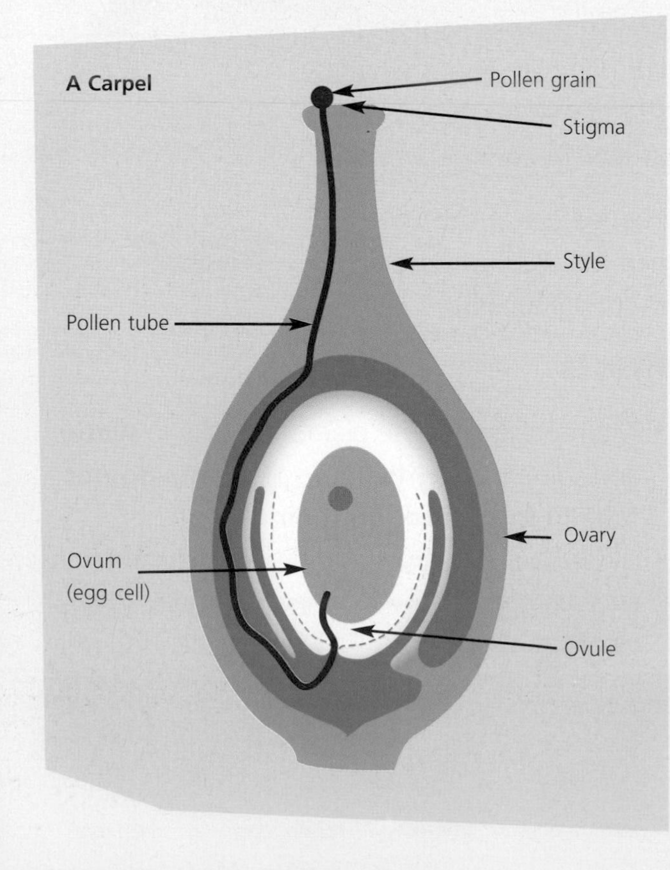

Seed Production

A seed is formed from a **fertilised ovule**. It is a tiny life support system which protects and nourishes the new plant in its early days of development. An ovary may produce just one seed or many seeds. The example here produces a single seed:

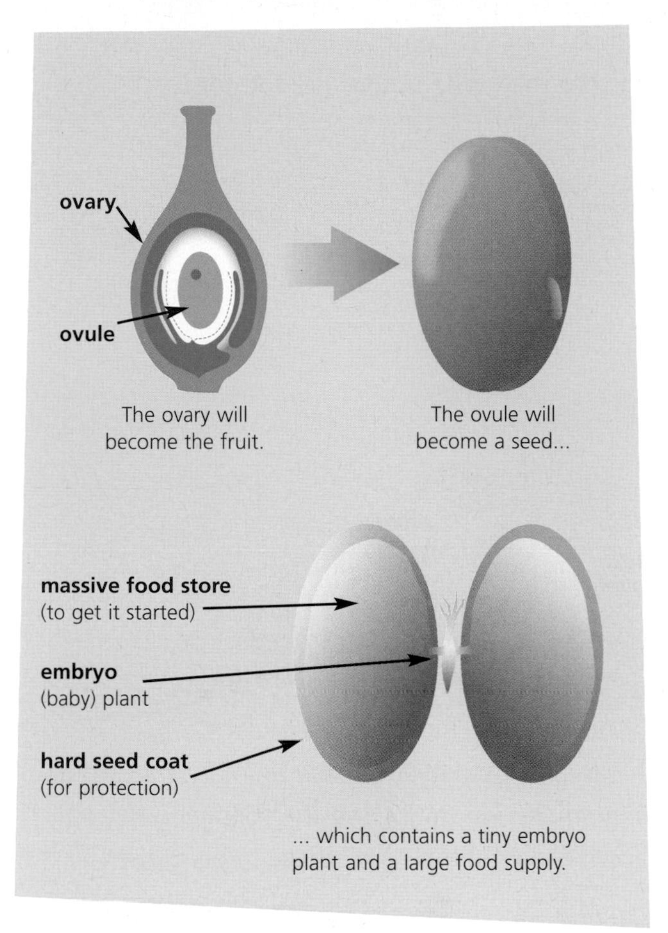

Seed Dispersal

It is important that seeds are **dispersed** (scattered) over a wide area so that the new young plants will not be over-crowded and in competition with each other. Seeds can be dispersed by **wind** or by **animals**.

Sycamore
Wings enable the seeds to travel a greater distance from the parent plant.

Dandelion
Parachutes float on the wind.

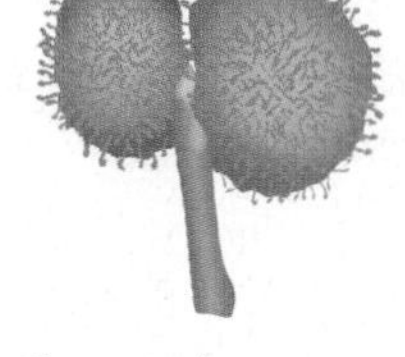

Cleavers (goosegrass)
Hooks become attached to animals.

Gooseberry
Eaten by animals but the seed passes straight through them.

Hazelnut
Stored away and forgotten by squirrels.

26 Decide which of the following would be dispersed by wind, and which by animals.

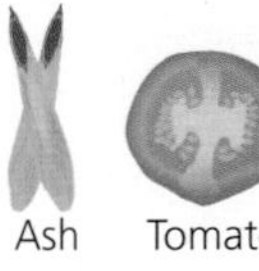
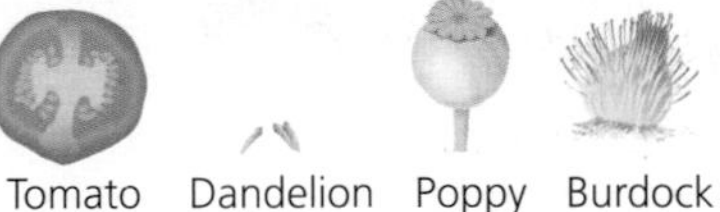
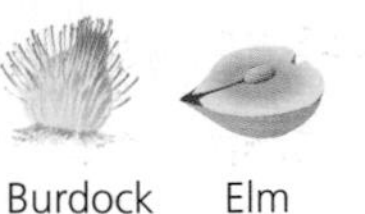

Ash Tomato Dandelion Poppy Burdock Elm Rosehip

Germination

This is when a seed starts to grow into a new plant. For **germination** to occur, the seed must have certain conditions, otherwise it will simply lie in the soil. The three things the seed needs are:

27 Isn't it strange that, although plants need light, seeds don't need light in order to germinate? Can you explain why it is an advantage that the seed does not need light?

1 **Enough water** – seeds are very dry and must absorb water to start growing.

2 **Oxygen** – seeds need oxygen to begin growing.

3 **Correct temperature** – it depends on the plant, but most need some warmth.

Life Processes and Living Things

Making and Using Keys

A key is made up of a series of questions, each one of which divides a group of organisms into two smaller groups. This carries on until each individual is in a group of just one and can therefore be identified. It's a very clever way of identifying animals and plants quickly, and of organising the huge variety of animals and plants into groups.

You would probably be asked to identify the garden organisms using this key, for example:

- Take organism C, and go to 'START'.
- Answer the question 'Has it got legs?'. (The answer is 'yes' so follow the 'YES' path).
- Answer the next question 'Has it got more than 3 segments?' (The answer is 'yes').
- Follow the 'YES' path and you can't go any further than woodlouse, i.e. the answer!

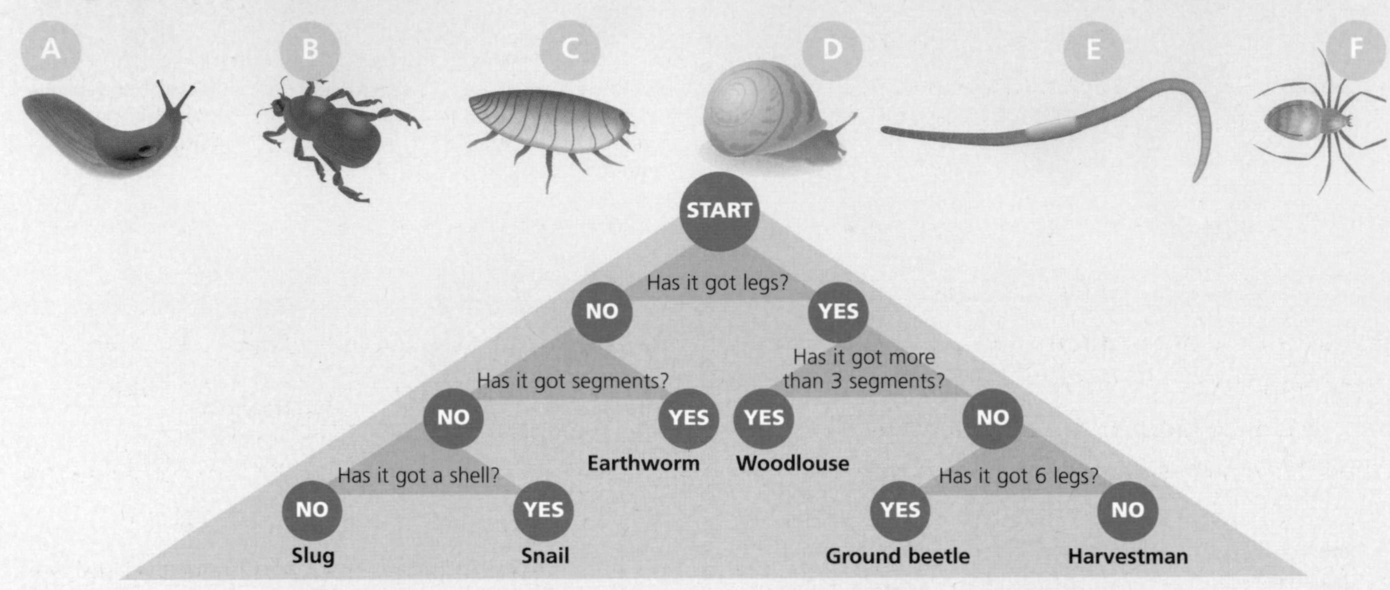

28 Now identify the other organisms A, B, D, E and F.

We can also use keys to place animals into groups. For example, we might use the following key to place these 6 animals into these large groups.

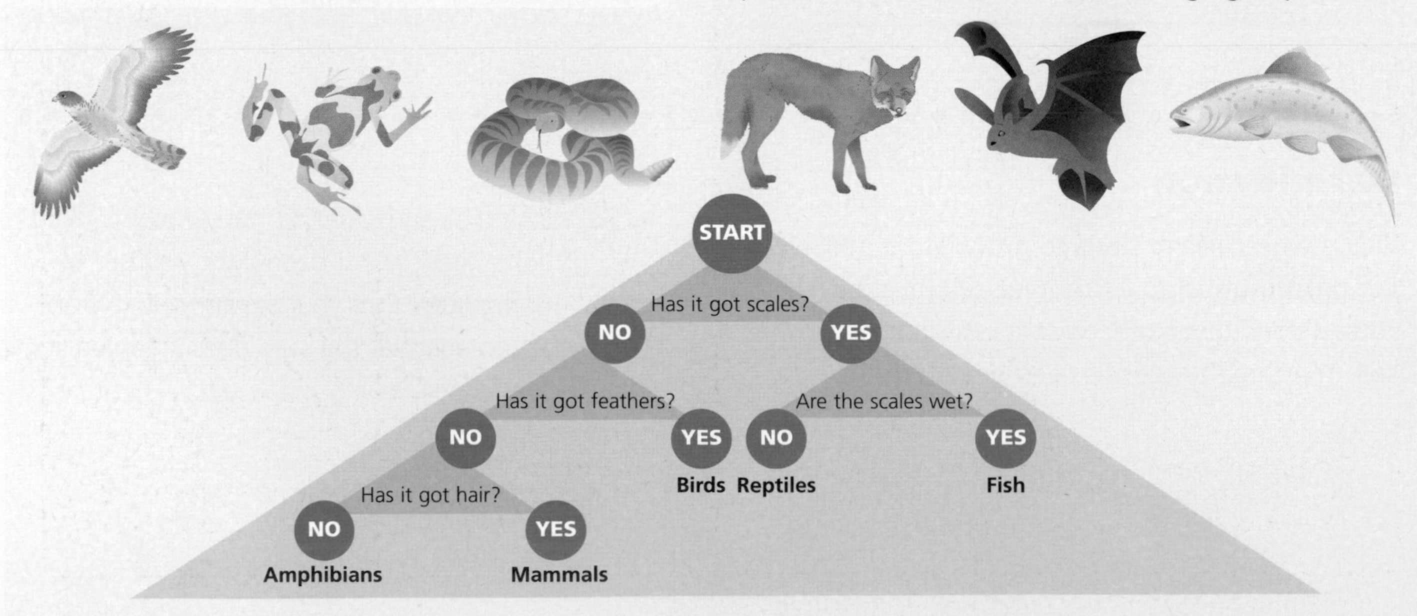

29 Think of 10 different animals with backbones and try to classify them into their groups, using this key.

30 Pick six of your friends in class and see if you could make a key to identify them.

Habitats

A **habitat** is the particular type of area in which an animal or plant lives. The habitat must supply **food**, **oxygen**, **water** and **shelter**.

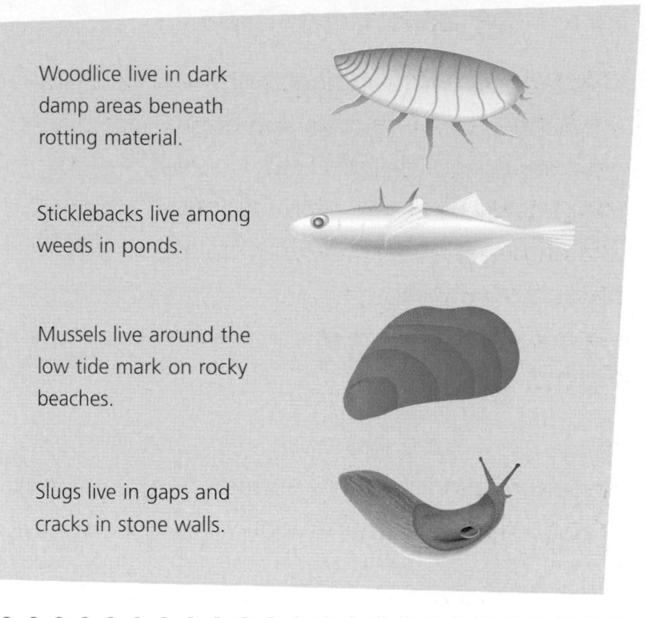

31 Write down 5 more examples of different habitats.

32 **a)** Write down the types of animals or plants which may live in these habitats.
b) Describe how you could do a fair test to find out whether woodlice prefer damp or dry conditions.

Adaptation to Environment

For an animal or plant to survive it must be **well adapted** to the conditions in its habitat (i.e. its **environment**). In other words it must have special features (**adaptations**) which make it perfectly suited to where it lives. (See table below.)

The environment is a delicate, fragile thing which, without human interference, is capable of looking after itself and the organisms in it. Humans, therefore, have a responsibility to show consideration for the environment and the living things in it.

Polar Bear	Camel	Cactus	Sparrow Hawk
• Thick layer of fat for insulation and storage. • Thick waterproof fur for insulation. • Large feet to distribute weight over snow and ice. • White colour to blend in with surroundings.	• Big fat store in hump. • Large feet for soft sand. • Can take in large amounts of water in one go. • Sand coloured for camouflage. • Doesn't lose much water through sweat or urine.	• Leaves are reduced to spines to reduce water loss... • ... and to keep grazing animals away. • Swollen stem stores water. • Widespread roots to increase absorption area.	• Streamlined shape and powerful wing muscles enable it to reach high speeds to catch prey. • Excellent eyesight for hunting. • Powerful beak and talons ('claws') for seizing prey.

33 Write down how you think the following animals and plants are adapted to their environment.

a) a frog
b) a mole
c) a grass snake
d) a shark
e) an oak tree
f) moss

Life Processes and Living Things

Feeding Relationships

In a particular environment there may be many different types of animals and plants. The plants get their energy directly from the Sun. Animals get their energy by eating plants or other animals. So, in a particular area, there may be lots of different feeding relationships.

Food Chains

Food chains are a way of showing the different feeding relationships in a certain area. If we look at the animals in the countryside around us, we might find the following food chains. The arrows show the way food is moving, i.e. the grass is eaten by the rabbit, and the rabbit is eaten by the fox.

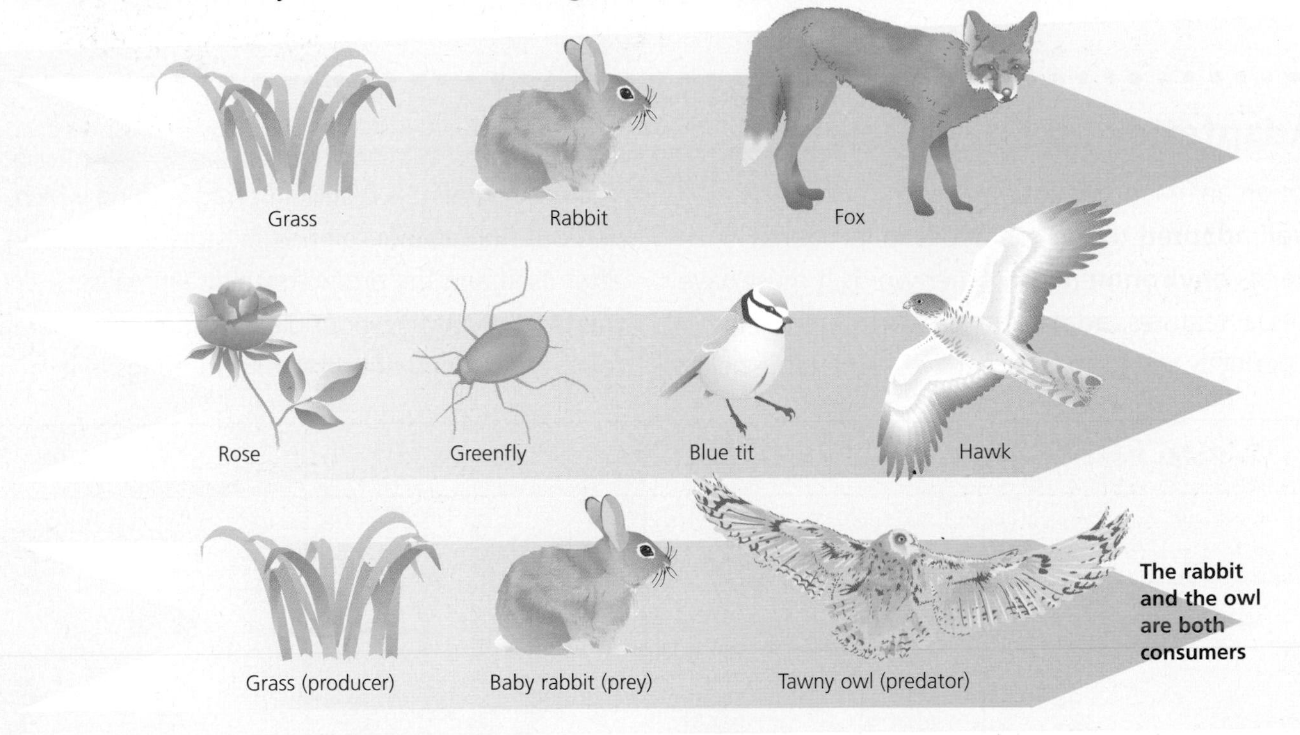

If one animal eats another then the animal doing the eating is the **predator** and the animal being eaten is the **prey**.

You will have noticed that all these food chains start with a **green plant**. We call green plants **producers** because they produce the food for the rest of the food chain. The rest of the organisms in the food chain are called **consumers** because they consume other organisms in the chain.

When an organism dies, **microorganisms** such as bacteria break it down in the same way as they break down waste. This releases nutrients back into the environment so they can be recycled. These microorganisms are called **decomposers**.

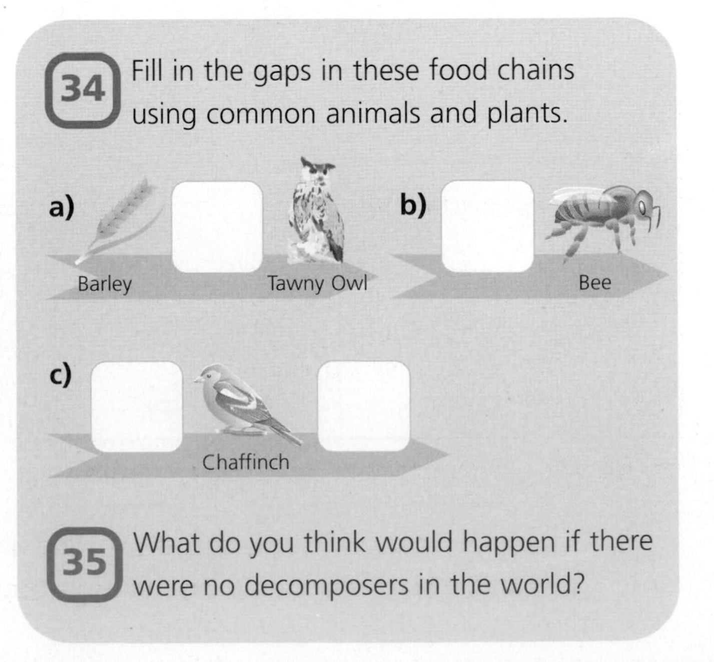

34 Fill in the gaps in these food chains using common animals and plants.

35 What do you think would happen if there were no decomposers in the world?

Materials and their Properties

Describing Materials

Different materials have different **properties**. We need to be able to use words to describe these properties. Here are some of the most common ones:

Hardness

- A hard material doesn't change shape very easily and will dent or scratch a softer material. For example, iron is harder than wood.
- Some examples of hard materials are **diamond** and **steel**.

iron hammer — dent — wood — wooden mallet — iron

Iron makes a dent in wood... but... wood doesn't make a dent in iron

Strength

- A strong material is very difficult to break when it is stretched, or squeezed or twisted.
- Some examples are **reinforced concrete** and **steel**.

reinforced concrete pillars

steel girder to support a roof

Flexibility

- A flexible material can be bent easily without breaking.
- Some examples are **rubber** and most **plastics**.

plastic credit card

Elasticity

- An elastic material can be stretched but will go back to its original shape when it is released, as long as it isn't stretched too far.
- Some examples are **rubber bands** and **metal springs**.

Attraction to a Magnet

- A few materials (iron and steel) are attracted to a magnet.
- All other materials are not attracted.

Toughness and Brittleness

- A tough material is difficult to break by hitting it with another object, e.g. **wood**, **most metals** and **some plastics**
- A brittle material breaks easily if it is hit, e.g. brittle materials such as **ceramics, glass** and **some plastics**

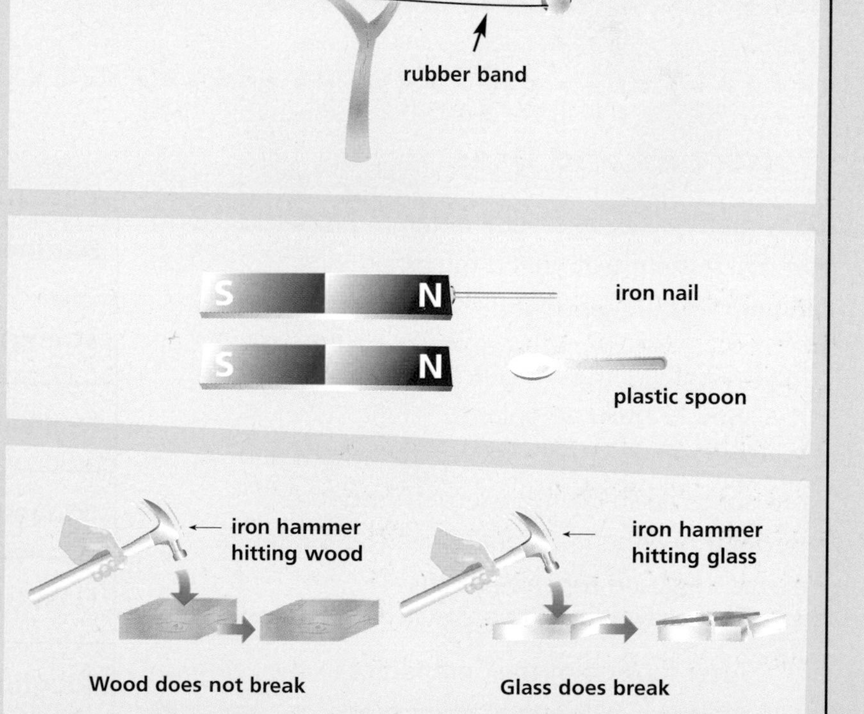

1. For each of the properties listed above, name three household objects which possess that particular property.

2. Think of other words to describe properties of materials.

Materials and their Properties

Grouping Materials

If we wish, we can sort materials into groups which have similar properties. Look at the objects below. We could group them as shown.

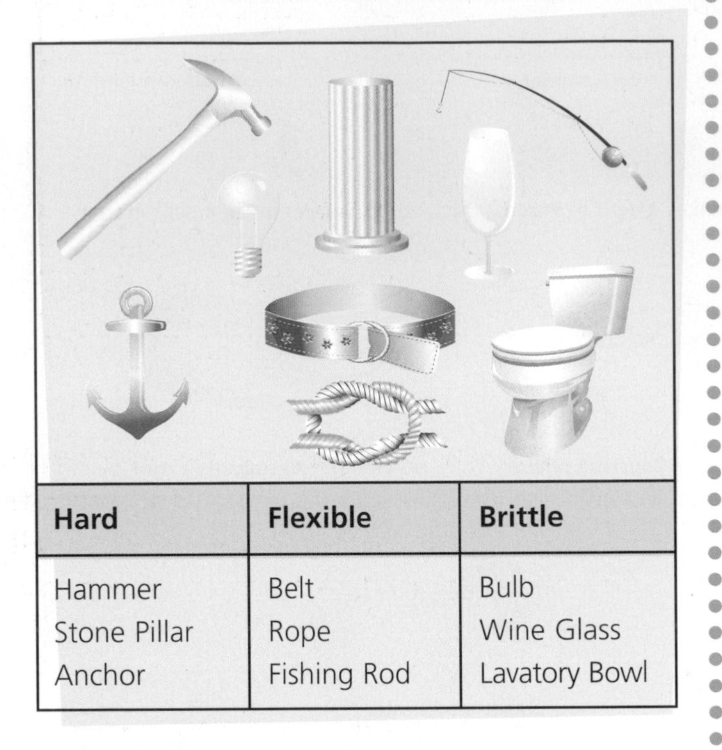

Hard	Flexible	Brittle
Hammer	Belt	Bulb
Stone Pillar	Rope	Wine Glass
Anchor	Fishing Rod	Lavatory Bowl

You can probably think of other ways of grouping them, such as 'glass materials' or 'metals', etc.

Classifying Materials

It is possible to put materials into much bigger groups called classes. These classes can be different depending upon who's doing the classifying (sorting out).

MATERIALS

- **Textiles and Fibres** e.g. cloth and string
- **Glass** e.g. mirrors, wine glasses
- **Paper** e.g. cardboard
- **Stone** e.g. statues
- **Plastic Materials** e.g. ruler, pencil sharpener
- **Natural Materials** e.g. wood, leather
- **Elastic Materials** e.g. rubber
- **Brittle Materials** e.g. china, porcelain cups
- **Metals** e.g. church bells, girders

3 Try to group the following products under the headings in the table opposite.

a) A credit card **b)** A football
c) A T-shirt **d)** A coffee mug
e) An archer's bow **f)** A knife

Add one other object to each class.

Properties and Uses

Many materials have several different properties that make them well suited to certain jobs. Look at this table opposite:

- Because aluminium is light, tough and strong it is used to build aeroplanes.
- Because wood is quite strong, fairly light and has some flexibility it is used for furniture.
- Because polythene is light, flexible and fairly elastic it is used for carrier bags.

4 After looking at their properties in the table opposite, try to think of the different uses of:

a) Wood **b)** Rock
c) Iron **d)** Aluminium
e) Paper **f)** Polythene

	Wood	Rock	Iron	Aluminium	Paper	Polythene
Hardness	✓	✓✓	✓✓✓	✓		
Strength	✓✓	✓✓✓	✓✓✓	✓✓✓		
Flexibility	✓				✓✓✓	✓✓✓
'Magnetic'			✓✓✓			
Elasticity						✓✓
Toughness	✓	✓	✓✓✓	✓✓✓		
Brittleness		✓✓✓				
'Lightness'	✓			✓✓✓	✓✓✓	✓✓✓

Materials and their Properties

Thermal Insulators

Grace decided to see if she could make tea cool down more slowly. She tried wrapping mugs of tea in different materials, and timing how long they took to cool to room temperature. Her results are shown in the table opposite.

- Bubble wrap and wool were best at stopping the tea cooling down. They are good **thermal (heat) insulators** because they don't let heat pass through them very easily.
- Another way of saying this is that they are **bad conductors of heat**.
- Most fluffy, furry or fibrous materials (made up of fibres) are good insulators because they trap air, which is a good insulator.

Good insulating materials can keep things cool as well as keeping things hot.

- Good **thermal insulators** include plastic, wood, glass, air, fibres.
- All metals are good **thermal conductors**.

Material	Time taken for tea to reach room temp
Bubble Wrap	90 minutes
Wool	90 minutes
Aluminium Foil	70 minutes
Newspaper	80 minutes
Nothing	60 minutes

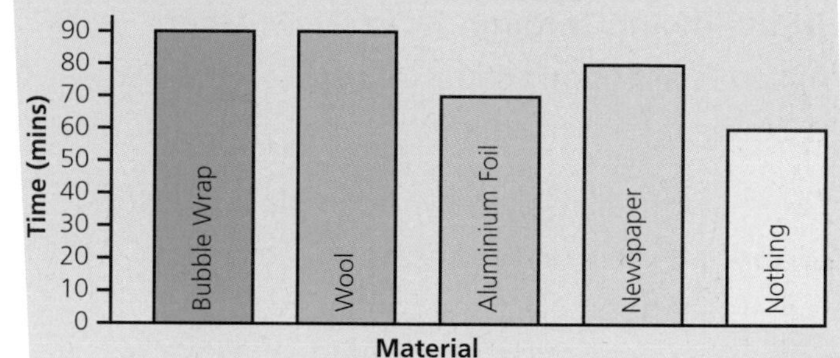

5 What would Grace have to keep the same in her investigation in order to make it a fair test?

6 Why do saucepans often have handles made of wood or plastic, when the rest of the pan is metal?

Some Examples of Thermal Insulation

7 **a)** Write down four other examples of good insulators. Draw them if you can.

b) Explain how wearing lots of different layers of clothes keeps you warm in winter.

Materials and their Properties

Electrical Insulators and Conductors

A good **electrical conductor** is a substance which **allows electricity to flow through it** easily. The opposite of an electrical conductor is an **electrical insulator**, which **stops electricity from flowing through it**. To see whether materials are good conductors we can use the equipment shown alongside.

Good electrical insulators include **glass**, **plastic**, **wood**, **air**, and **rusty metals**. All non-rusty metals are good electrical conductors.

However, you should remember that water can change insulators into conductors. In other words, if an object is wet it can allow electricity to flow through it. This is one reason why you should never handle electrical equipment (even switches) with wet hands!

8 Draw three household items which are good electrical conductors, and three which are good electrical insulators.

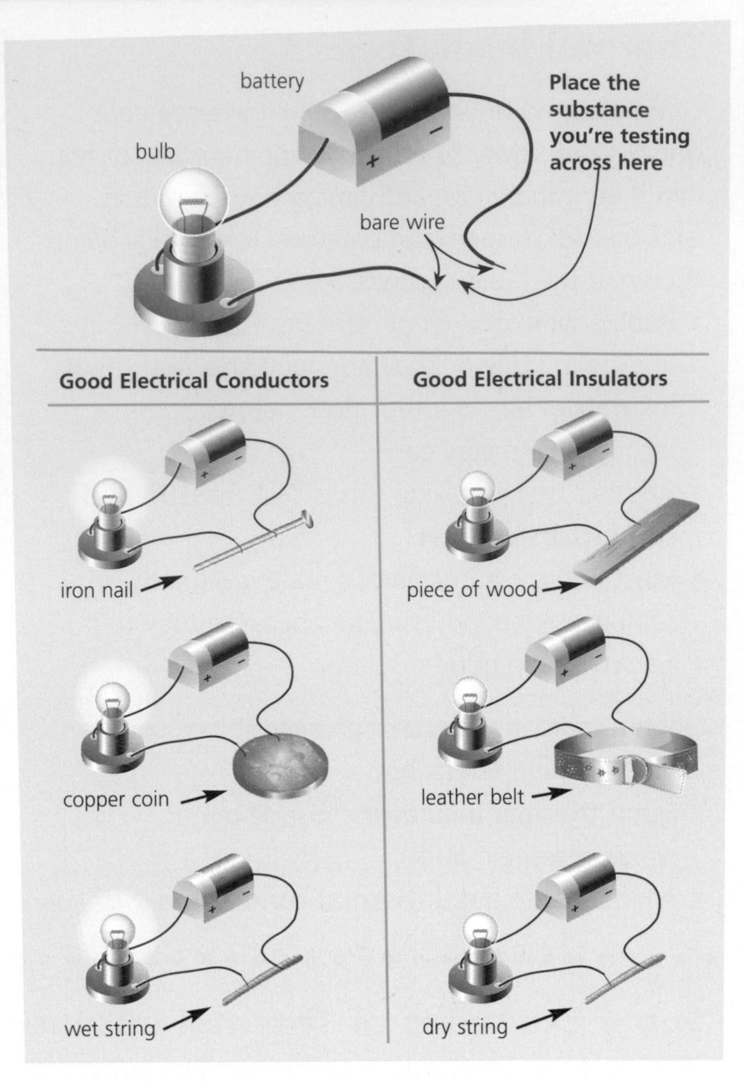

Use of Electrical Insulators and Conductors in the Three-Pin Plug

Nearly all **electrical appliances** are supplied with electricity by a **cable** connected to a **three-pin plug**, both of which make use of materials that are conductors and insulators:

- The **cable** is made from an insulator such as **plastic** or **rubber**.
- The **wires** are made from a conductor such as **copper**.
- The **pins** are made from a conductor such as **brass**.
- The **casing** is made from an insulator such as **plastic**.

9 Why would it be dangerous to plug a wet plug into a socket?

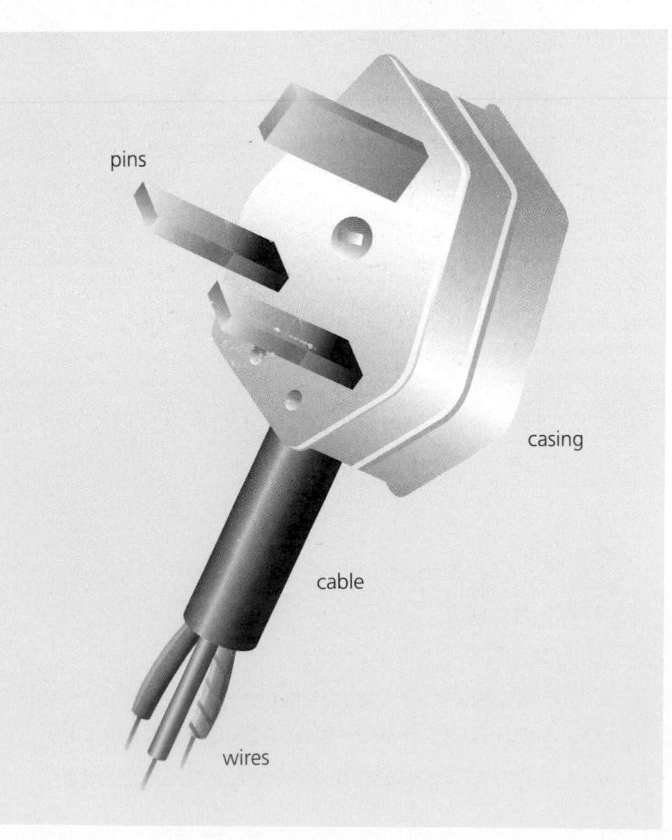

Materials and their Properties

Rocks

Rock exists naturally beneath all surfaces. Even your school playground – if you go deep enough. However, there are many different kinds of rock and they all have their own special characteristics. This is good for us because we can use them for different things.

polished e.g. marble for decoration

waterproof e.g. slate for roofing

hard wearing e.g. granite for building

soft e.g. sandstone for ornamental carvings

If rock isn't easily available then man-made building materials are used, e.g. bricks.

Characteristics of Rocks

We can group rocks roughly into three types based on their characteristics:

1. **Crumbly rocks which are permeable**, e.g. sandstone, chalk
2. **Hard rocks made of crystals which are not permeable**, e.g. granite
3. **Hard, smooth rocks made of crystals in layers. They are not permeable**, e.g. marble, slate

Permeable means the rock will allow water to pass through it (see table opposite).

Soil

Soil is formed from broken-down rock particles together with dead animal and plant material. How much water and air there is in the soil depends on the type of rock particle it is made from. There are basically three types: sandy soil, clay soil and equal mix of sand and clay soil.

Of course, some soils don't quite fit into these groups, e.g. 'peaty' soils which are full of dead plant material and 'stony' soils which are full of (yes, you've guessed) small stones.

- We can look at whether the particles in a soil sample are big or small by first drying the soil, then sieving it.
- We start with a sieve with big holes and then put the soil which passes through it into a sieve with smaller holes, and so on.

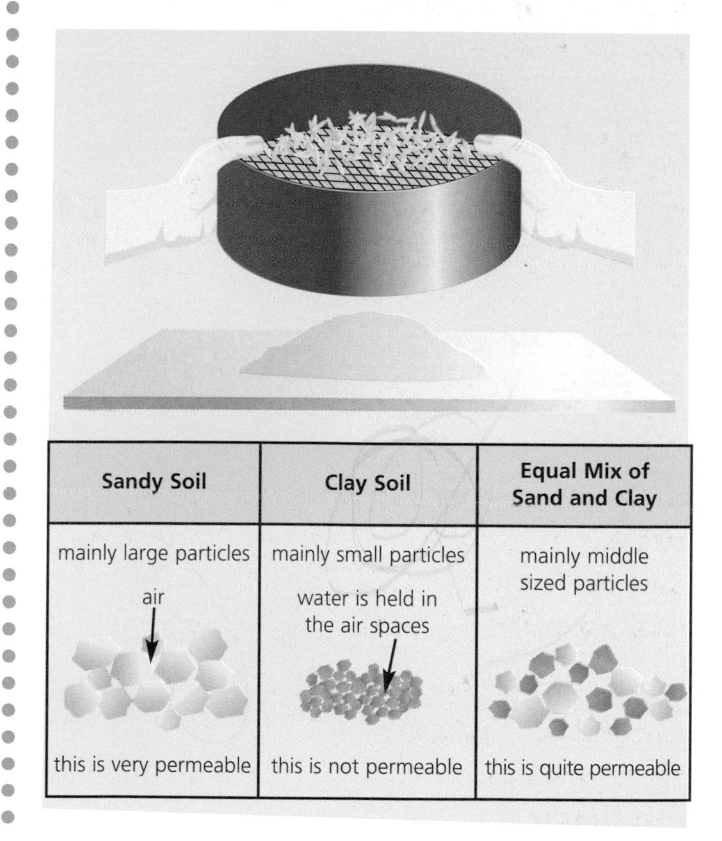

Sandy Soil	Clay Soil	Equal Mix of Sand and Clay
mainly large particles air this is very permeable	mainly small particles water is held in the air spaces this is not permeable	mainly middle sized particles this is quite permeable

Pupils cut drinks bottles in half to make funnels. They put gauze over the neck of the funnel and placed different soil samples in each one. They poured water into each funnel and got the results shown here.

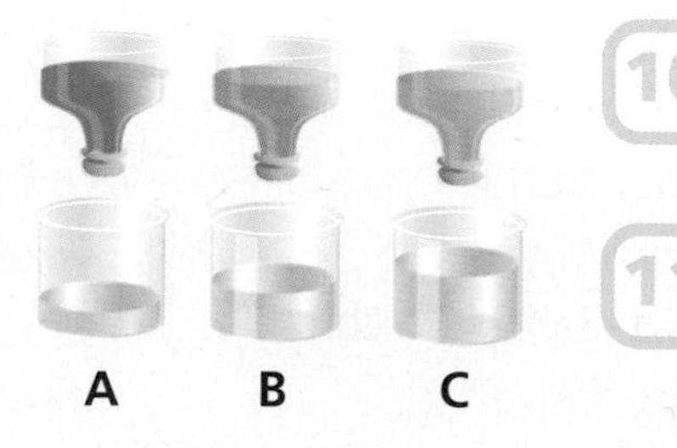

10 Can you name the sandy, clay, and equal sand and clay soils?

11 Which two things would you have to keep the same in order to make this a fair test?

Materials and their Properties

Solids, Liquids and Gases

All materials are made of matter and can exist as either **solids**, **liquids** or **gases**. These are called the three **states of matter**, and they have different properties which help us to recognise them.

What we need to know is:

- How easily does a substance **flow**?
- Does it keep a fixed **shape**?
- Does it keep a fixed **volume**?

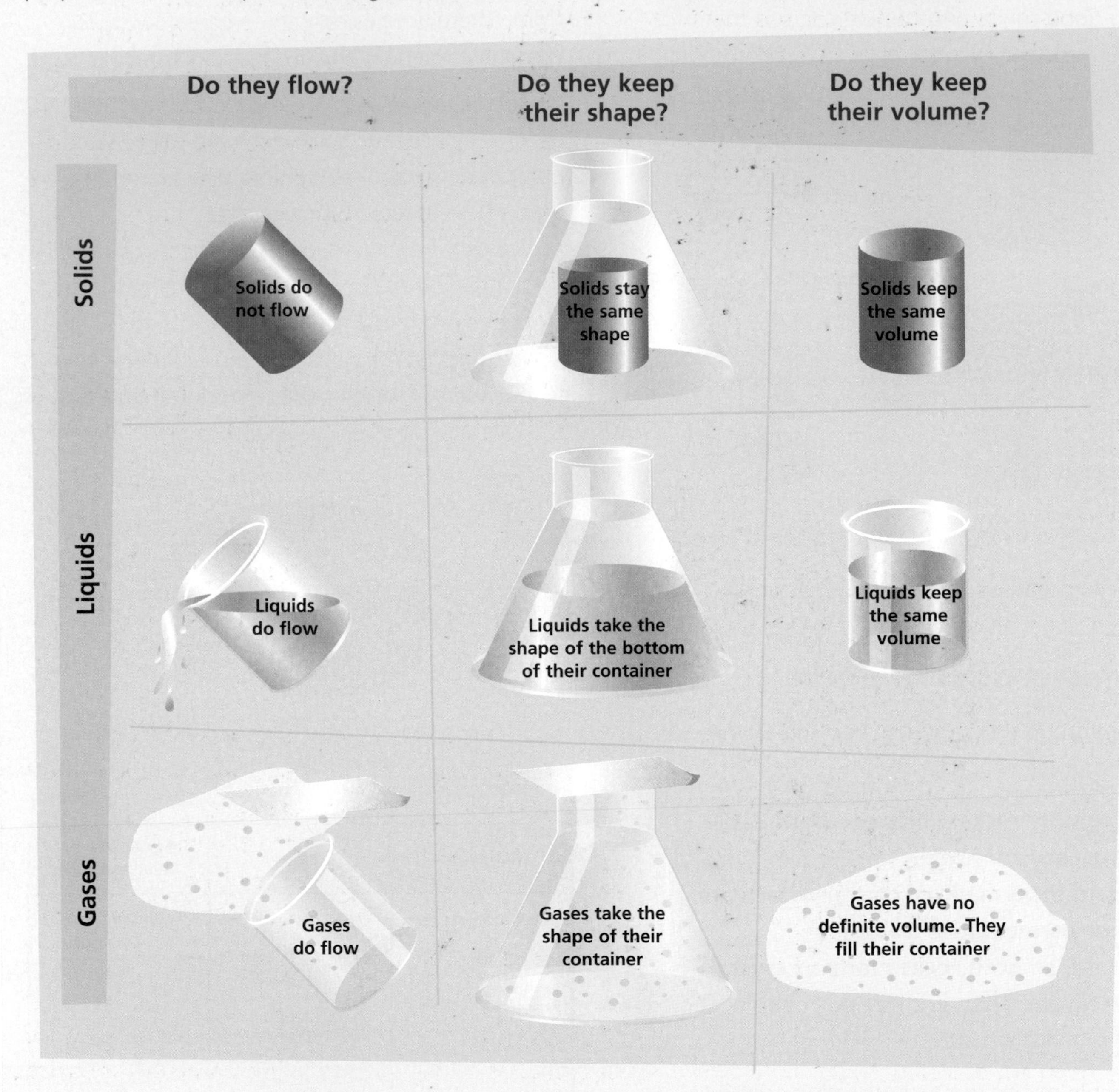

12 **a)** For each of the following, say whether it is a solid, liquid or gas: steam from a kettle; a school desk; air; tomato sauce; an ice cube; a bowl of sugar.
b) Which of these doesn't really fit the properties listed above? Explain why.
c) Could you name another substance which behaves like your answer to **b)** above?

13 Complete the following sentences:
If it doesn't flow it must be a ....
If it flows it could be a .... or a .... If it keeps the same volume it could be a .... or a .... If it takes the shape of its container it must be a .... If it stays the same shape it must be a ....

Materials and their Properties

Measuring Temperature

We measure temperature so that we can compare how hot or cold different objects are. Temperature is measured in **degrees Celsius** (°C) using a **thermometer**.

- The thermometer on the left below is measuring 20°C, which is roughly 'room temperature'.
- Whenever you want to measure the temperature of something, you must always make sure that the bulb of the thermometer is in it or touching it. (See thermometer on the right below.)

Warming Up and Cooling Down

Have you noticed that when you leave a nice cold drink standing around too long, it warms up? Or, if you leave a hot drink for a while it cools down?

Suriya decided to investigate these two things. First she took a freshly made mug of tea and put a thermometer into it. She decided to measure the temperature every 10 minutes, and mark it on a graph. After this she took a can of cola which had been in the refrigerator for a short while, and measured the temperature of this every 10 minutes.

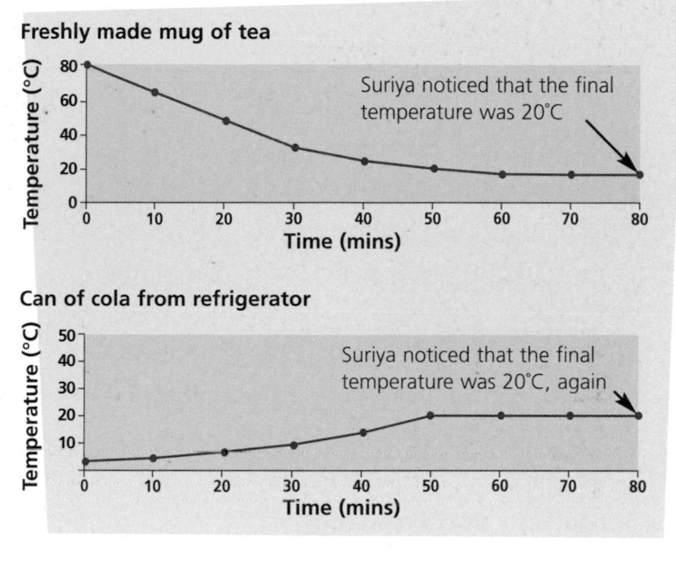

Because the final temperature of the two drinks was the same as the temperature of the room, Suriya came up with the conclusions below:

- Hot things cool down until they are at the same temperature as their surroundings.
- Cool things warm up until they are at the same temperature as their surroundings.

14 Estimate the reading on the thermometers in these pictures.

a) b) c) d)

15 Now mark each of your estimates on the thermometers below.

a) b) c) d)

16 If Suriya had put a good heat insulator around the cola and the tea above, how would this have affected cooling and warming?

Materials and their Properties

Reversible Changes

We can do things to substances, which can cause them to change. Many changes can easily be reversed and are called **reversible changes**.

Reversible changes produce no new materials. Some examples of reversible changes are shown in the table below:

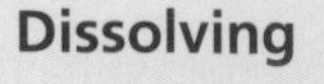

Dissolving
If we dissolve something in water to form a solution (see p.31), we can get it back by evaporating all the water off.

Boiling and Condensing
Water will boil at 100°C to form steam (water vapour). When the temperature of this steam falls, it turns back into water.

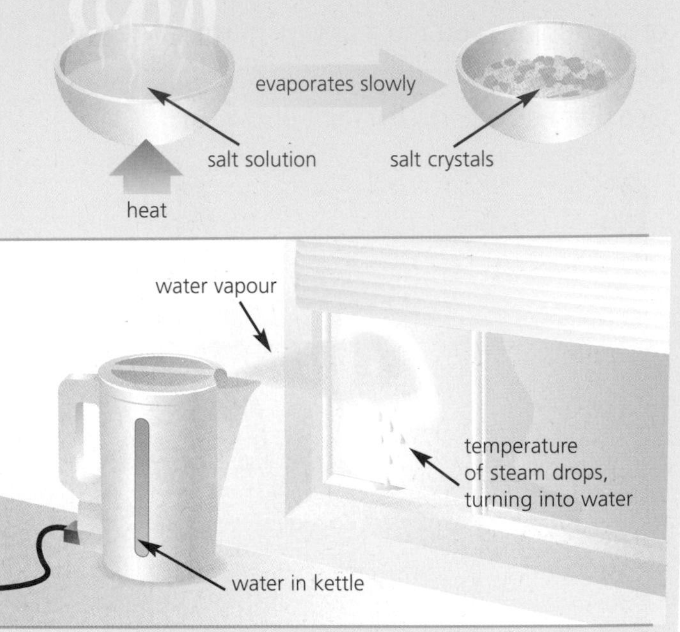

Melting and Freezing
Ice will melt if left at normal room temperature but can easily be changed back to ice by putting it in the freezer.

Ice tray from freezer — Ice cubes — water — water in ice tray to freezer — Ice cubes

Evaporation
This is like boiling, where water turns into water vapour. However, evaporation occurs naturally much more slowly and at much lower temperatures.

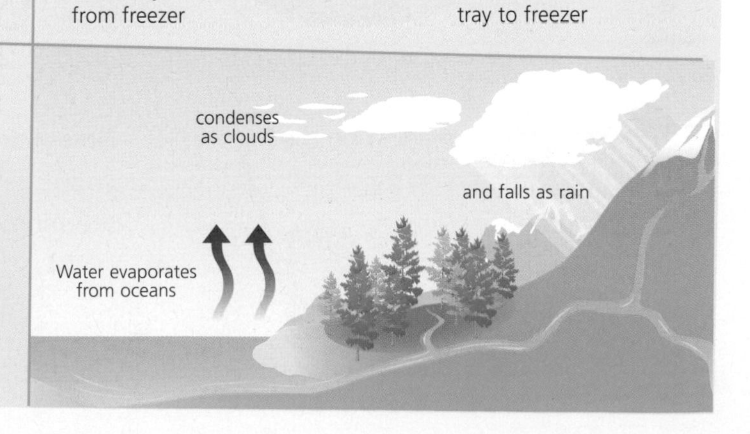

17 Which of the following are reversible changes?

a) Candle wax melting
b) Letting off a firework
c) Mixing water-colour paint
d) Wood burning
e) Frying an egg

Irreversible Changes

Some changes happen when materials are mixed, which cannot be reversed. We call these changes **irreversible changes**. **Irreversible changes produce new materials** Some examples of irreversible changes are shown in the table below:

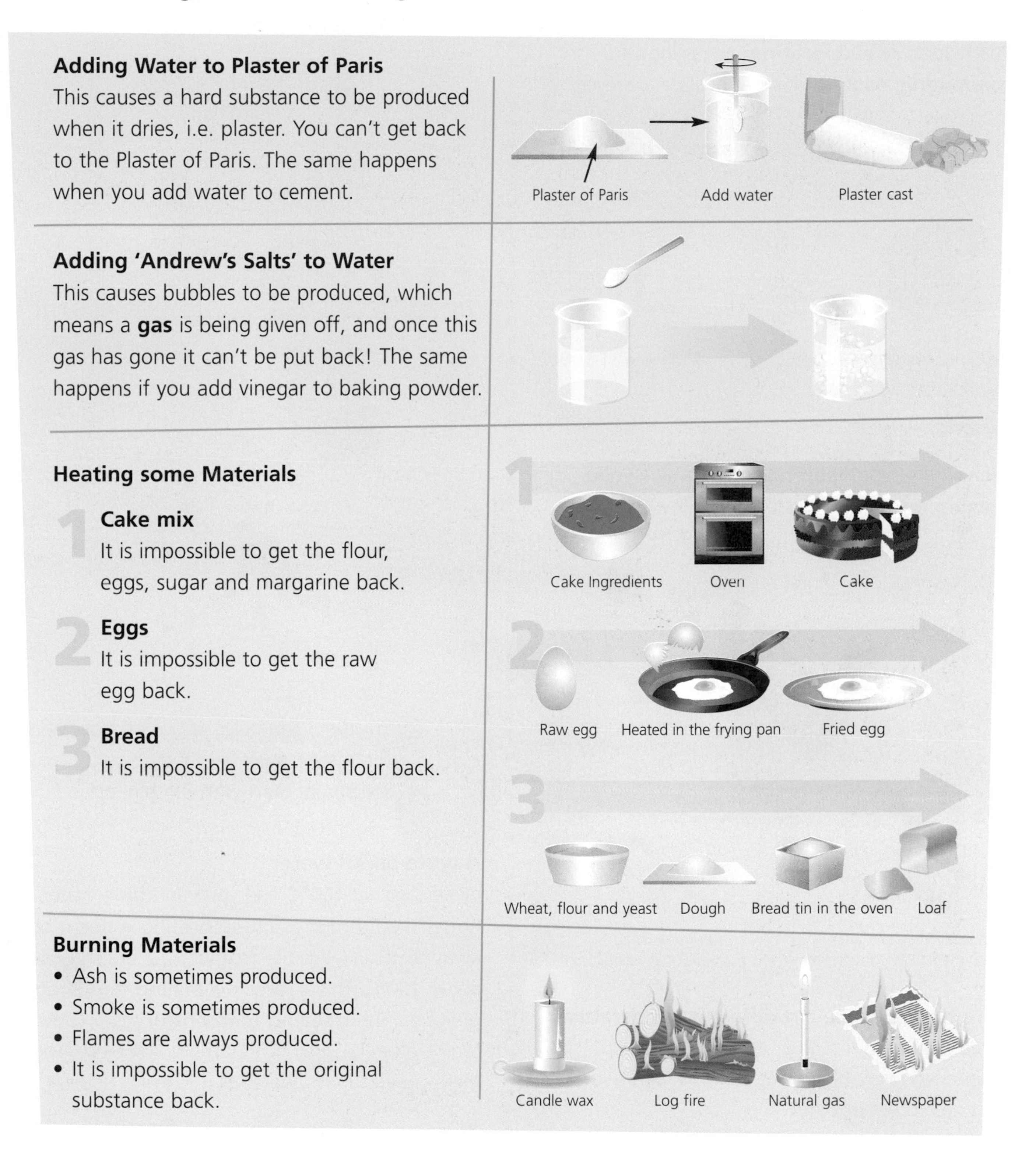

Adding Water to Plaster of Paris
This causes a hard substance to be produced when it dries, i.e. plaster. You can't get back to the Plaster of Paris. The same happens when you add water to cement.

Adding 'Andrew's Salts' to Water
This causes bubbles to be produced, which means a **gas** is being given off, and once this gas has gone it can't be put back! The same happens if you add vinegar to baking powder.

Heating some Materials

1. **Cake mix**
   It is impossible to get the flour, eggs, sugar and margarine back.
2. **Eggs**
   It is impossible to get the raw egg back.
3. **Bread**
   It is impossible to get the flour back.

Burning Materials

- Ash is sometimes produced.
- Smoke is sometimes produced.
- Flames are always produced.
- It is impossible to get the original substance back.

18 Which of the following are irreversible changes? **a)** Dissolving salt in water **b)** Freezing water **c)** Sticking things together using superglue. **d)** Making bricks from clay **e)** Setting a firework off

Materials and their Properties

Changing State

Most substances can exist as solids, liquids, or gases (see p.24), and can change state from one to another. Let's look at the example of water:
The reverse of **melting** is **freezing** (or solidifying).
The reverse of **evaporating** (or boiling) is **condensing**. All these changes of state are reversible.

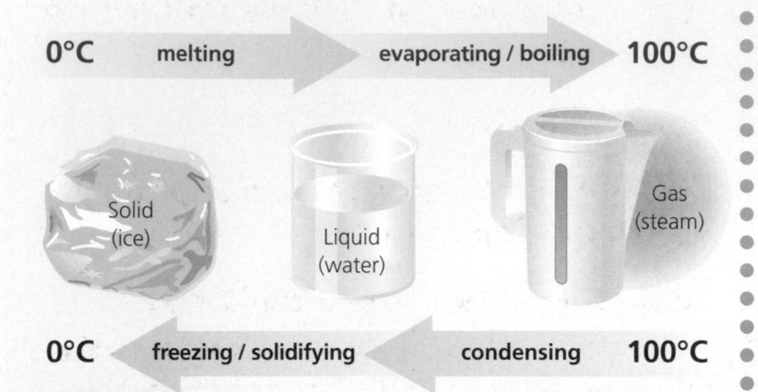

Melting

We use the word **melting** to describe a **solid turning into a liquid**. Here are a few examples:

Wax has melted and run down the side of the candle.

Molten lava (melted rock) runs down the side of a volcano.

Chocolate has melted and become 'runny'.

An ice lolly melting after being taken from the freezer.

Liquid iron being poured into a mould.

Different solids melt at different temperatures. Some melt at low temperatures (e.g. ice) but others need very high temperatures, and a lot of heat has to be 'put into' the solid.

19 Put the 5 examples above in order of the temperature at which they melt. Start with the one that melts at the lowest temperature.

Solidifying

We use the word **solidifying** (or **freezing**) to describe a **liquid** turning into a **solid**. Here are a few examples. **Different liquids solidify at different temperatures.**

Candle wax solidifies as it cools.

When hot molten gold cools it becomes solid again.

Water freezes at 0°C.

20 Put the 3 examples above in order of the temperature that they would solidify at. Start with the highest.

A word about water...
Water boils at 100°C and you can't have water hotter than this! If you keep heating water, it boils away to steam, but the temperature doesn't rise above 100°C. This is called the **boiling temperature** of water. The **freezing temperature** is 0°C. Room temperature is usually 20°C. The graph below shows the temperature of water as it is being heated.

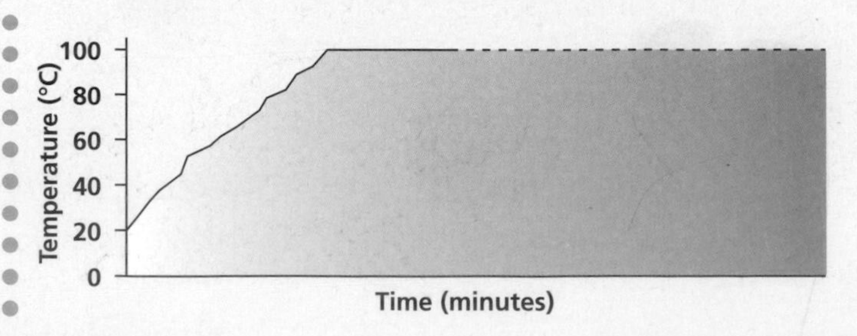

Evaporation

We use the word **evaporation** to describe a **liquid turning into a gas**. Some examples are shown below:

Liquid turning into a Gas	
	A wet hand print on a blackboard disappears.
	Washing on a clothes line dries out.
	Water in a saucepan left on the hob will quickly boil away. Boiling is a very fast form of evaporation where there are always bubbles.
	Puddles on the school playground dry up.

Other liquids besides water evaporate. For example, nail varnish remover, perfume and aftershave.

Speeding up Evaporation

If you were given a beaker full of water and wanted it to evaporate as fast as possible, you might try the following...

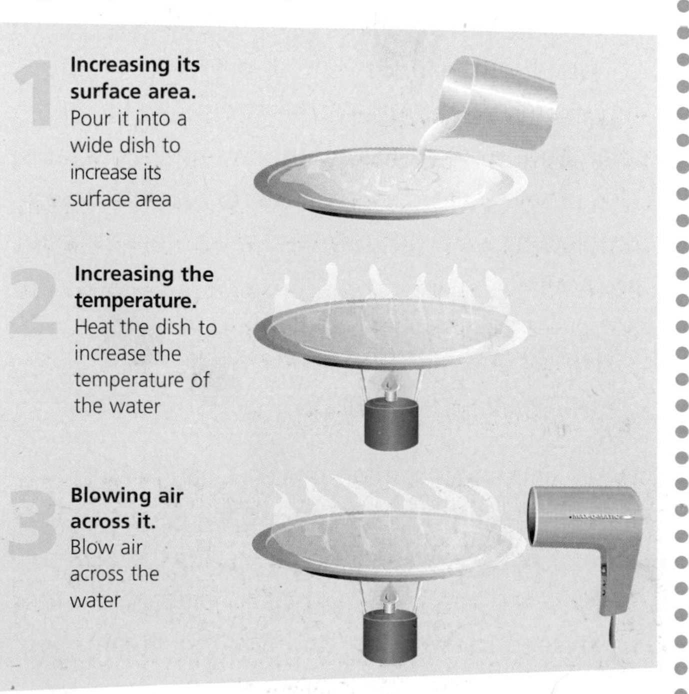

Modern appliances use these three ideas to help dry things more quickly. For example...

- hairdryers
- tumble dryers
- rotary clothes line.

21 Explain why a hairdryer and a tumble dryer would speed up the drying process.

Condensation

We use the word **condensation** to describe a **gas turning into a liquid**.

Condensation is the reverse of evaporation. Water vapour (i.e. water as a gas) **changes state** to become liquid water. This is usually caused by the water vapour hitting a cold surface and therefore becoming colder. Some examples are shown below:

Gas turning into a Liquid	
	Water vapour in the air you breathe out condenses on a cold mirror.
	Steam from a kettle condenses into water on a cold window.
	Water vapour in the air condenses on a cold drink can.

22 Explain why condensation often occurs in kitchens and bathrooms.

The Water Cycle

The water cycle recycles all the water on our planet using the processes mentioned on the previous two pages, i.e. evaporation, condensation, freezing and melting.

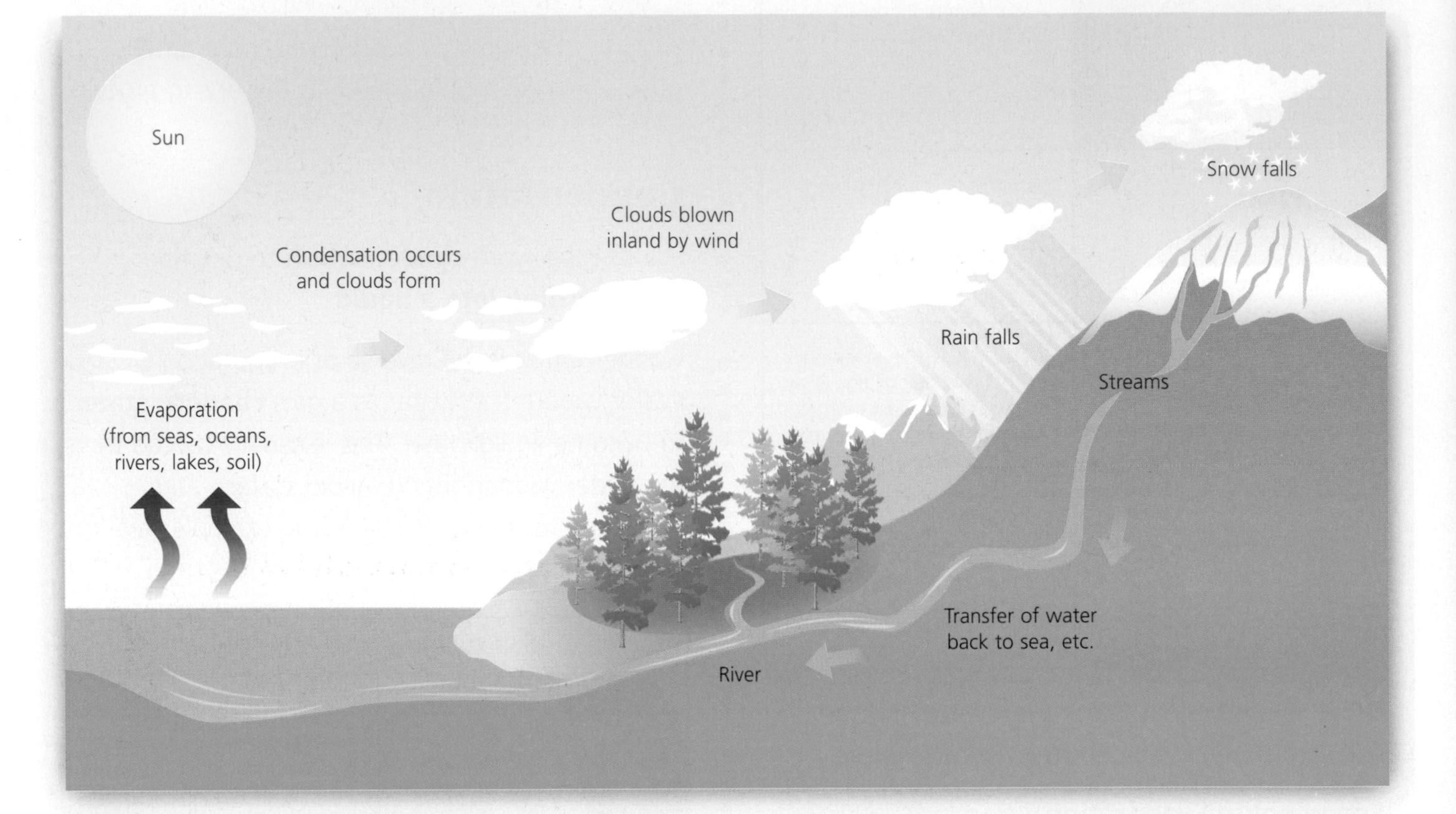

Evaporation in the water cycle:

Liquid → Gas (Water Vapour)

The water lying on the Earth's surface and in the rivers and oceans is constantly evaporating. This change of state from liquid to gas is caused...

- by heat from the Sun
- by wind blowing over the land and sea
- because the water is spread over a large surface (see p.29).

Evaporation happens faster on warm, windy days.

23 Imagine you are a drop of water. Tell the story of your journey around the water cycle from leaving the sea until you get back to the sea. Make sure you mention all the processes on this page.

Condensation in the water cycle:

Gas (Water Vapour) → Liquid

As invisible water vapour rises, it cools and condenses into clouds. Clouds are made up of tiny droplets of water. As the clouds are blown inland, they rise as they meet hills and mountains. This makes them cool even more, causing large droplets of water to form and fall as rain, or even as snow.

Melting and Freezing in the water cycle:

Solid ↔ Liquid

When snow falls in high places it can remain there for long periods of time because of the low temperature. This takes water out of the water cycle. When the snow eventually melts, the water is returned to the cycle, and flows in streams and rivers out into the sea.

Solutions

When a solid **dissolves** in a liquid, a **solution** is formed.

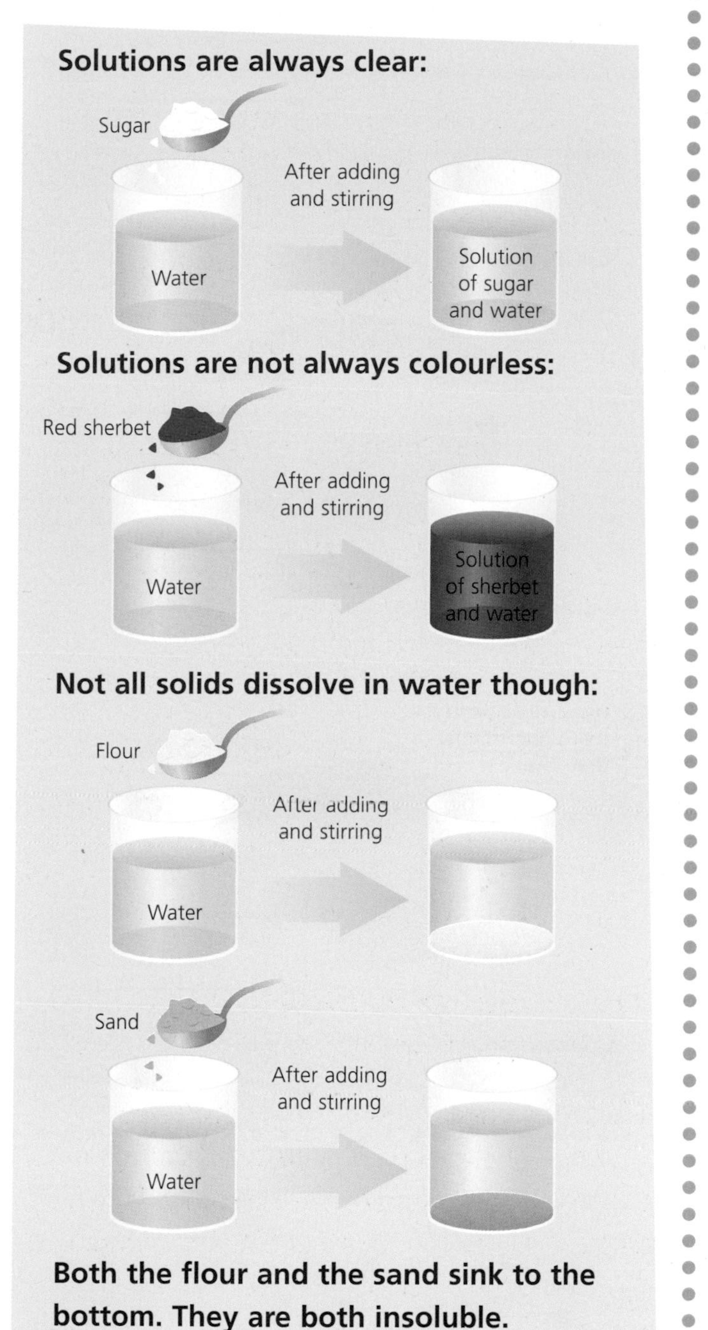

Making Solids Dissolve Faster

A great way to look at this is to think about dissolving sugar in a cup of tea!

The sugar will dissolve quicker if...

- **you have a bigger volume of tea:**
- **the tea is hotter:**

- **you add smaller particles of sugar:**

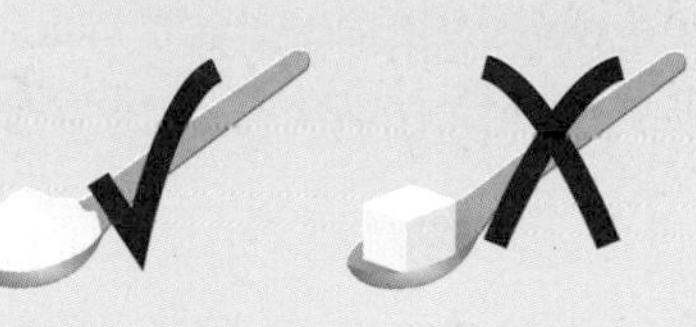

- **you stir the tea well:**

24 Which two of the following substances dissolve in water to form solutions?
a) Salt **b)** Chalk **c)** Sand **d)** Instant Coffee

25 Name three substances which are insoluble in water.

26 You are given a mixture of sugar and sand. What would you notice if you added this mixture to a beaker of water and stirred it?

27 Name four ways in which dissolving sugar in a cup of tea can be slowed down.

28 Plan an investigation into how temperature affects the speed at which sugar dissolves in water. Say which things you would have to keep the same to make it a fair test.

Separating Solids

If several solids are mixed up together, it is often possible to separate them again so that you end up with the things you started off with. For example, if you mixed up rice, dried peas, paper clips and sand you might separate them like this:

1. Use a magnet to pull out all the paperclips. Obviously you will have to spread the mixture out a little so that the magnet can pull all the paperclips out.
2. Use a sieve with holes just smaller than dried peas. The rice and sand will go through the holes in the sieve, but the dried peas won't! To make sure all the rice and sand goes through, you will have to shake the sieve thoroughly until you are left with just the peas.
3. Use a sieve with holes just smaller than rice. The sand will go through the holes in the sieve, but the rice won't! Again, to make sure all the sand goes through, you will have to shake the sieve thoroughly until you are left with just the rice.

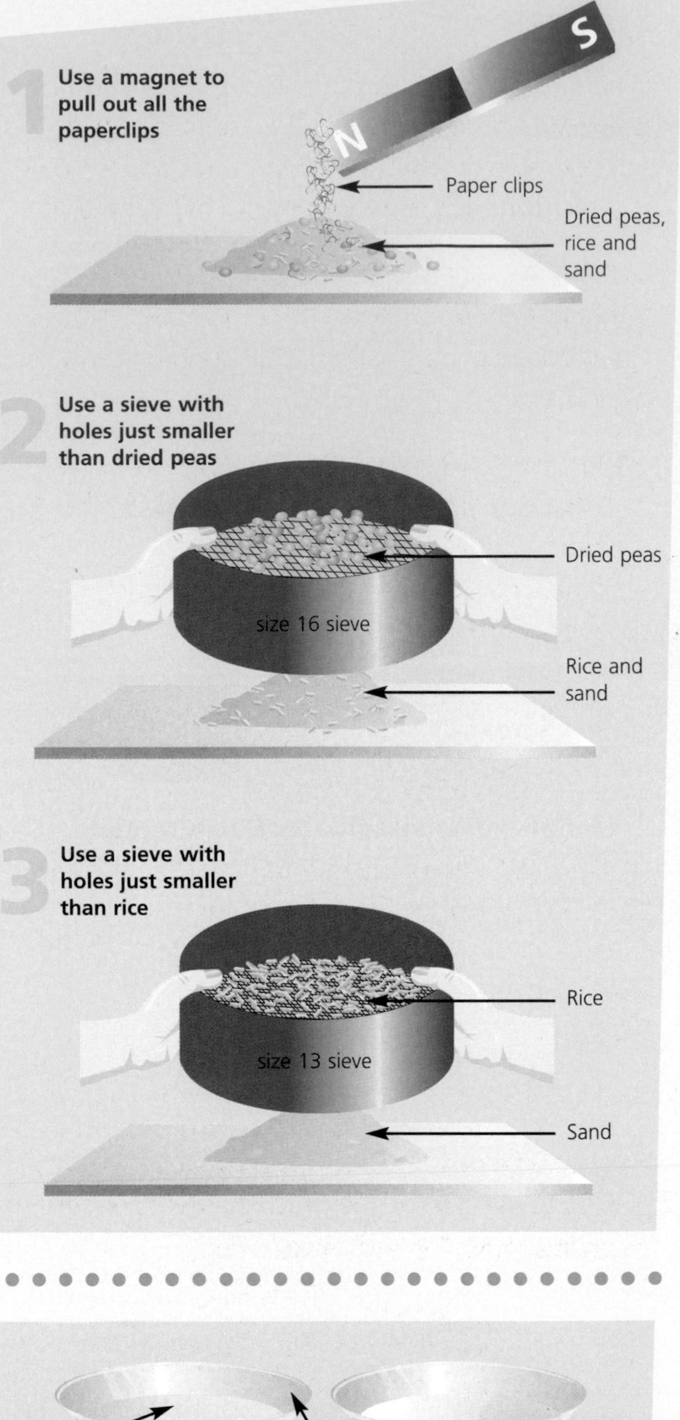

29 Explain how you would separate a pile containing 6 tennis balls, 200 nails, 150 small marbles, a lot of dried peas and even more rice!

Separating Undissolved Solids from Liquids

(See page 31 on dissolving.) Some solids such as sand and chalk don't dissolve in water, but their particles are very small and can't be easily removed by a sieve because the holes would be too big. So, we use a special type of 'sieve' – filter paper. If we look at filter paper under the microscope we can see it's full of tiny holes, which only allow water and **dissolved** substances through!

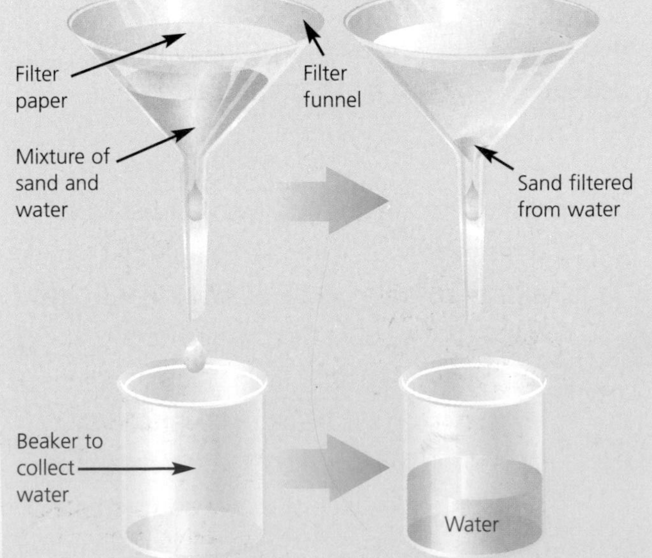

30 Explain why filtering would be no good for separating sand and chalk.

Separating Dissolved Solids from Liquids

Solids which dissolve form clear solutions (they may be coloured but they don't have any 'bits' in them), and **cannot be separated by filtering!**

Substances which are dissolved go straight through filter paper because the particles of the substance are smaller than the holes in the filter paper.

To separate the salt from the solution...

- leave it for several days to evaporate slowly at room temperature, or
- heat it gently if you want to evaporate the water off more quickly.

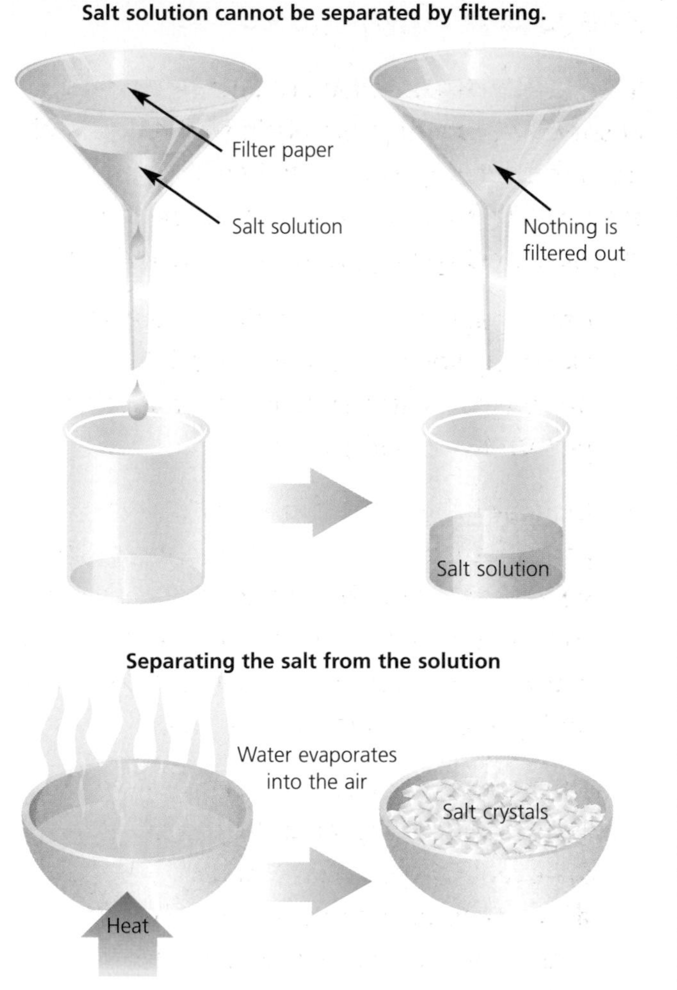

31 Which of the following could be separated by evaporation?

a) A solution of blue dye in water.
b) Salt and sugar both dissolved in water.
c) Lemonade and water.

A Big Separation Problem!

Suppose we had to separate a mixture of gravel, sand and salt, the sort of stuff you might put on roads in winter. This is what we'd do:

32 Describe what you might do to try to separate the substances in a shovel full of mud from the bottom of a pond.

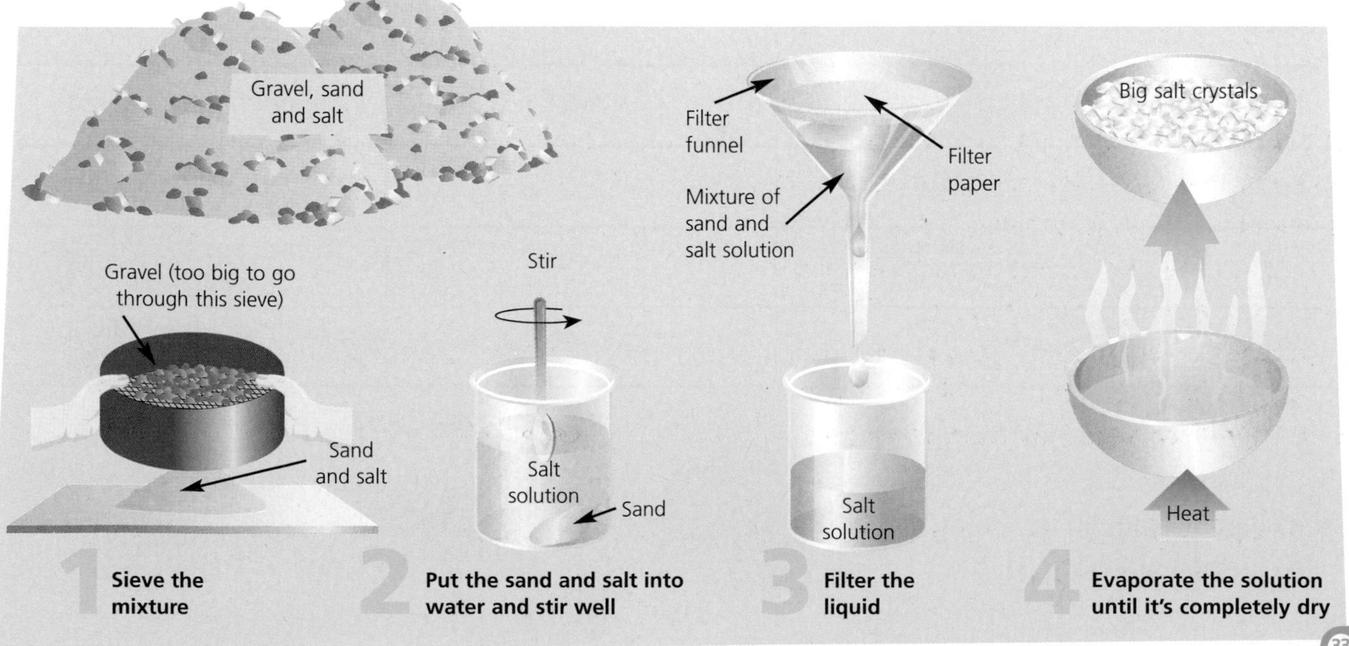

Physical Processes

Electrical Appliances

Electricity is very useful. At home or school, electricity is used to make lots of different appliances work. All appliances need electricity in order to produce **heat**, **light**, **sound** or **movement**. Four different appliances are shown alongside:

A lamp needs electricity to produce light.

A stereo needs electricity to produce sound.

A drill needs electricity to produce movement.

A kettle needs electricity to produce heat.

1 Name three other appliances that need electricity to produce each of the following: **a)** light **b)** sound **c)** movement **d)** heat.

2 Name one appliance that needs electricity to produce: **a)** light and sound **b)** sound and movement **c)** light and heat.

Simple Circuits

All appliances involve **circuits**. A very simple circuit has a **battery** or **power supply** (usually the **mains**) which supplies the electricity. This electricity then flows around the circuit through wires to a device, and causes the device to produce heat, light, sound or movement.

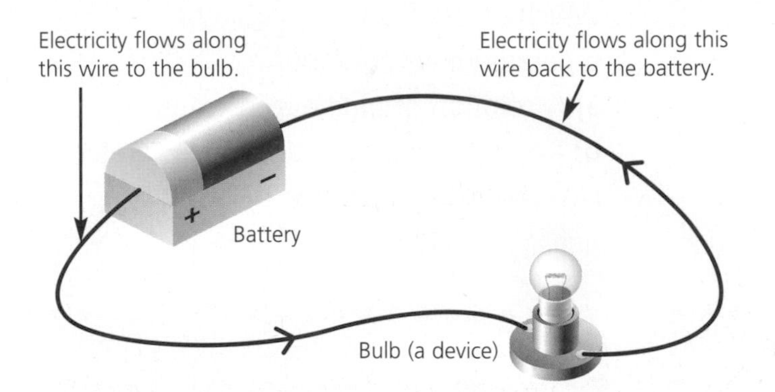

At school you will make up some simple circuits. You will use the following:

What it is	What it looks like	How we draw its symbol	What it does
Battery		or if there is more than one	Supplies the electricity
Bulb			Produces light
Motor		M	Produces movement
Buzzer			Produces sound
Switch			Switches the circuit on and off
Wires		or	Electricity flows along these to the devices

3 Draw the symbol for the following: **a)** Battery **b)** Bulb **c)** Motor **d)** Buzzer **e)** Switch **f)** Wire.

4 What... **a)** produces sound? **b)** supplies the electricity? **c)** produces movement? **d)** switches a circuit on or off? **e)** produces light?

Making Circuits Work

Electricity will not flow through a circuit which has a 'break' or gap in it. A **switch** is a device which can be used to 'complete' or 'break' a circuit so that devices can be switched on or off. This is very useful since it saves electricity, which saves us money! The table below shows some examples of circuits that won't work:

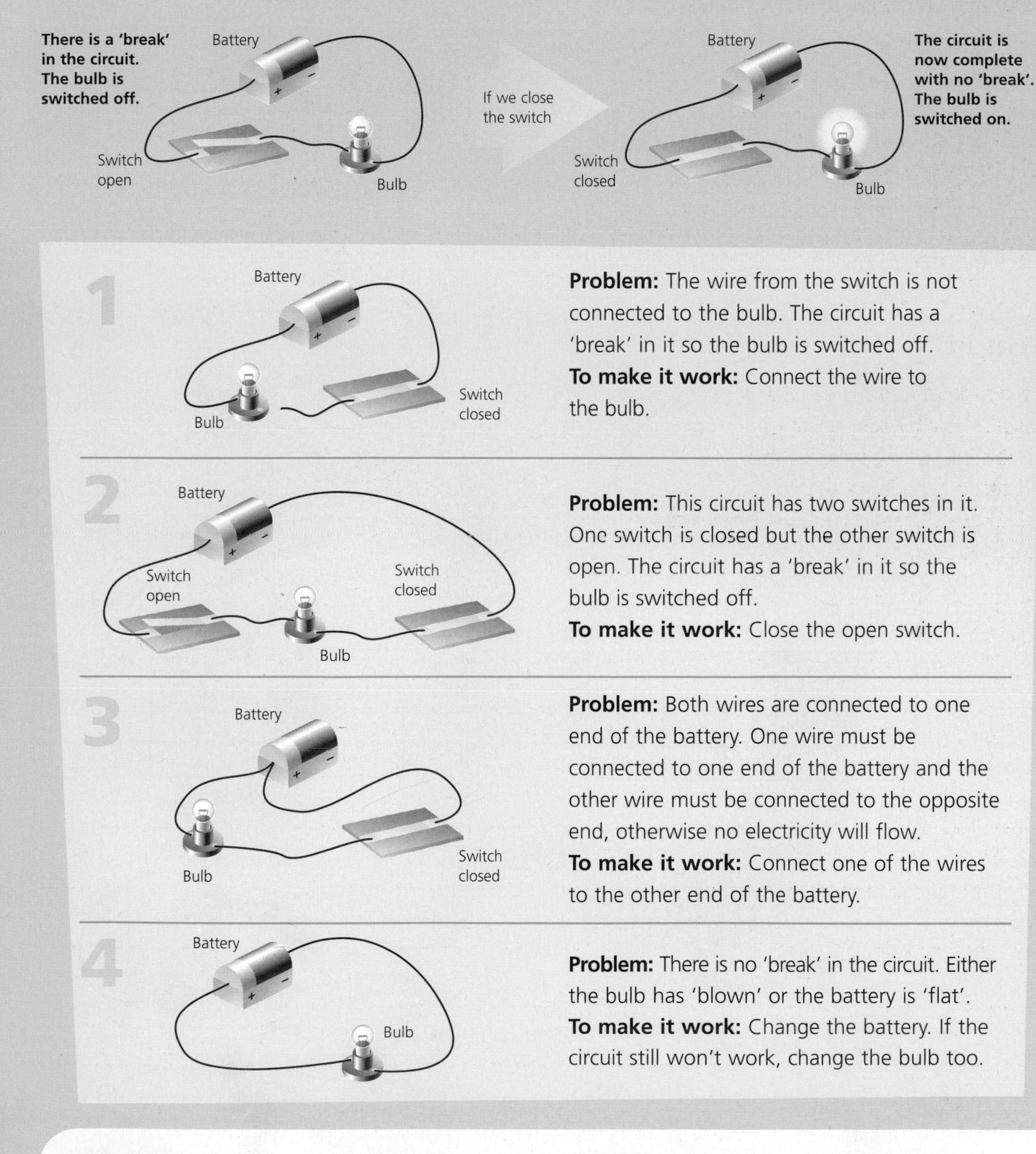

1

Problem: The wire from the switch is not connected to the bulb. The circuit has a 'break' in it so the bulb is switched off.
To make it work: Connect the wire to the bulb.

2

Problem: This circuit has two switches in it. One switch is closed but the other switch is open. The circuit has a 'break' in it so the bulb is switched off.
To make it work: Close the open switch.

3

Problem: Both wires are connected to one end of the battery. One wire must be connected to one end of the battery and the other wire must be connected to the opposite end, otherwise no electricity will flow.
To make it work: Connect one of the wires to the other end of the battery.

4

Problem: There is no 'break' in the circuit. Either the bulb has 'blown' or the battery is 'flat'.
To make it work: Change the battery. If the circuit still won't work, change the bulb too.

5 Make up and draw three other circuits that don't work. Explain why each circuit doesn't work and what needs to be done to make it work.

Physical Processes

Circuit Diagrams

Very often you will have to draw a diagram of a circuit you have set up. This drawing is called a **circuit diagram**. All circuit diagrams are drawn using symbols. Any circuit can be easily drawn providing you follow these two simple steps:

1. Draw your battery first. (This is your starting point.)
2. Work your way around the circuit from one end of the battery to the other end. Make sure you draw all the devices as you go along and don't forget the wires!

Here is a very simple circuit:

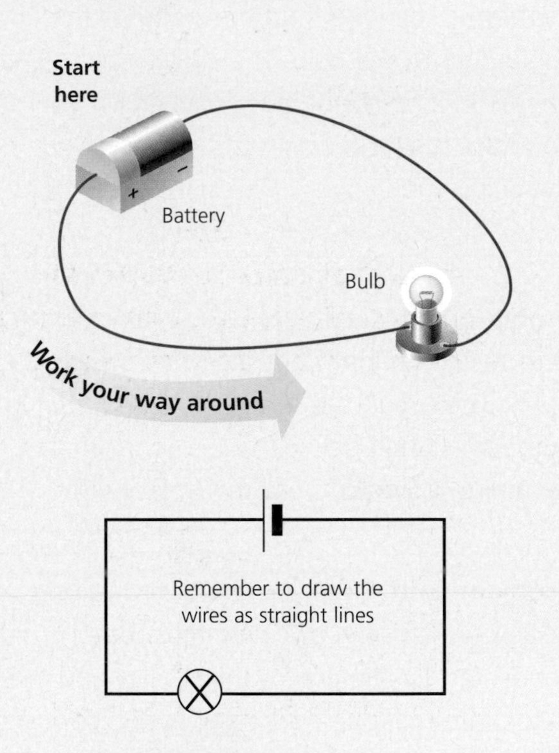

Here are some other examples:

Start here
Battery
Bulb
Switch
Work your way around

Remember to draw the wires as straight lines

Start here
Work your way around

Remember to draw the wires as straight lines

M

6 Draw circuit diagrams for the following circuits:

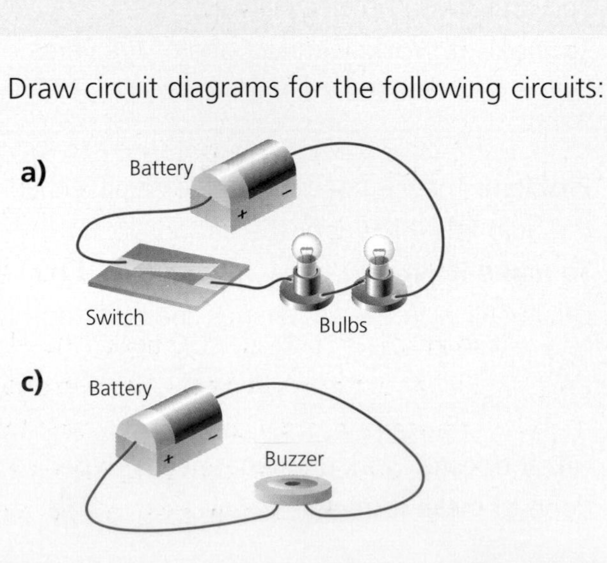

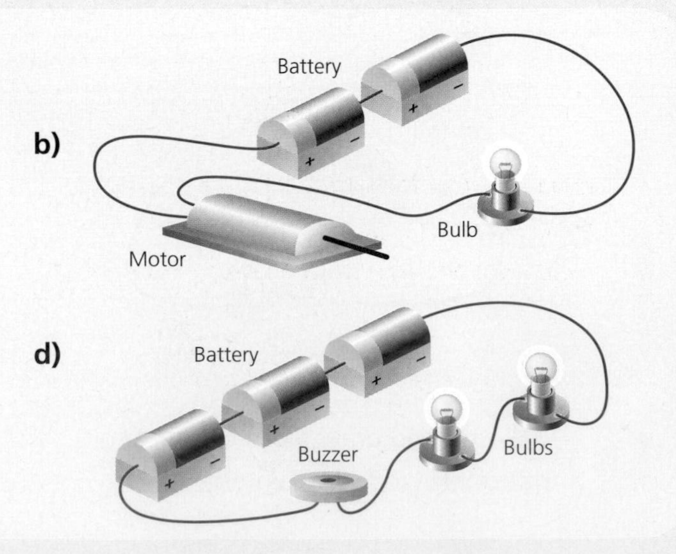

Electric Current

As we have seen, a battery is a supply of electricity. The flow of electricity in a circuit is called an **electric current**. A very simple circuit is shown opposite:

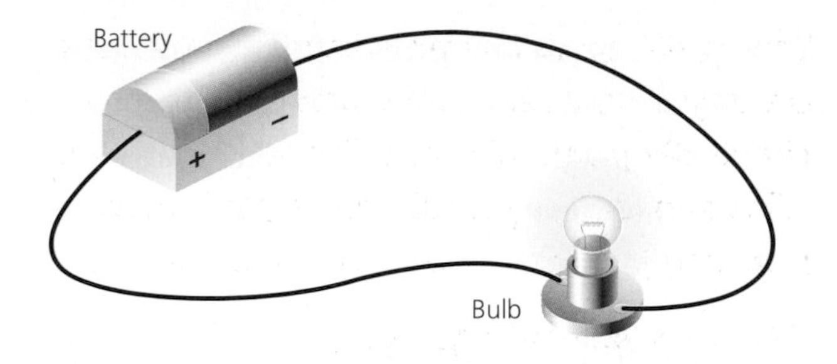

The brightness of a bulb in a circuit depends on how much current flows through the bulb.

The greater the current – the brighter the bulb

Decreasing Current & Brightness

Increase the number of bulbs
Two bulbs will cause less current to flow than one bulb.

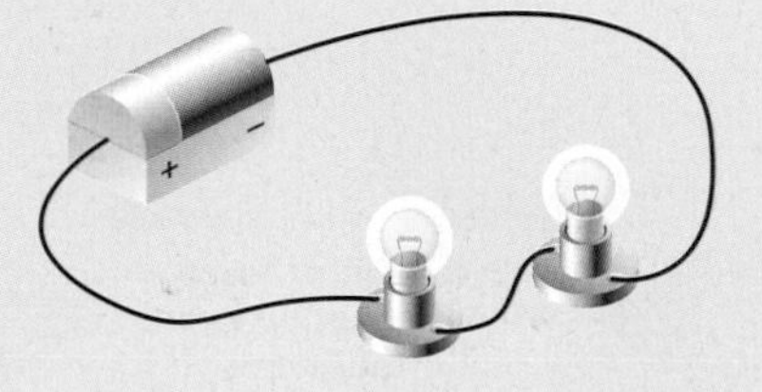

Use a different bulb
A higher-rated bulb will reduce the current flowing.

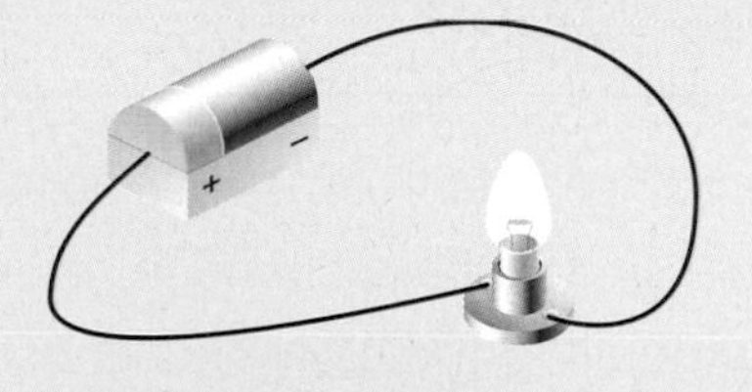

Use a thin wire
A smaller current flows in a thin wire.

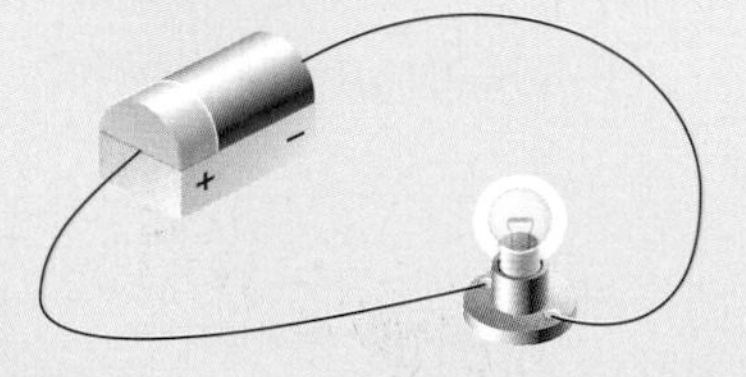

Increase the length of the thin wire
An even smaller current will flow if you increase the length of the thin wire.

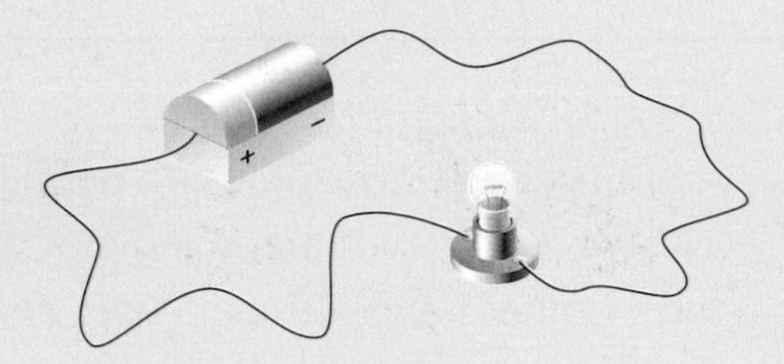

Increasing Current & Brightness

Increase the 'power' of the battery
i.e. use a more powerful battery. This battery makes a greater current flow in the circuit.

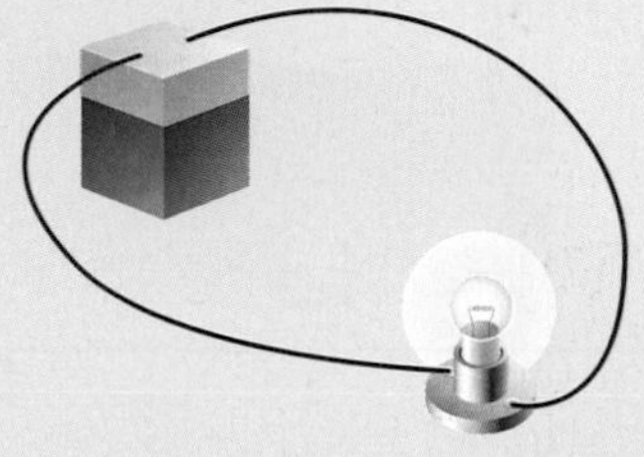

Increase the number of batteries
Two batteries will double the current compared with the diagram at the top of the page.

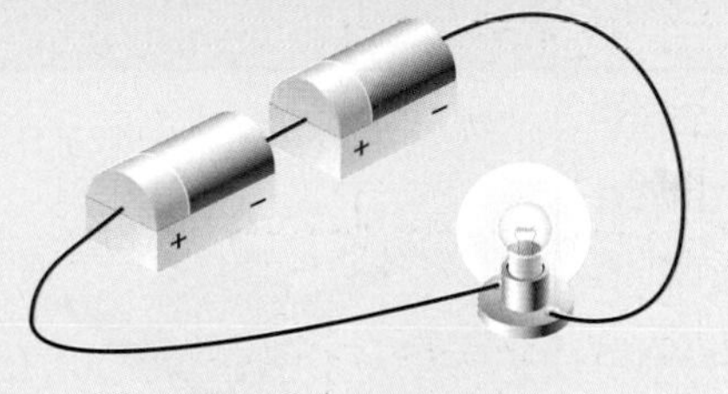

Use a thick wire
A greater current flows in a thick wire.

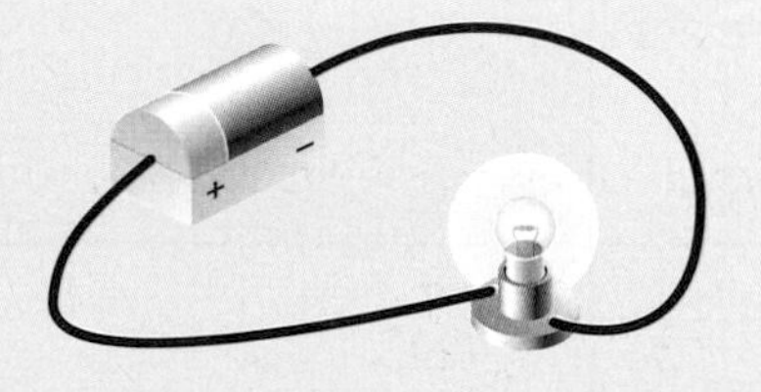

7. In an experiment to investigate the effect of using more batteries, what must be kept the same in order to make it a **fair test**?
8. What effect would changing the type of wire have on the brightness of the bulb?

Physical Processes

Forces

A force is a **push** or a **pull**. A force is drawn as a straight line with an arrowhead at the end to show the direction of the force. Forces are measured in **newtons** (N). The table below shows some typical forces in action.

This man is **pushing** the car. This man is **pulling** the cart.

A force called **friction** acts against the moving car.
A force called **weight** acts on the stationary girl.
A force called **air resistance** acts against the falling skydiver.
A force called **water resistance** acts against the moving boat.
A force called **upthrust** acts on the floating raft.

Forces Due to Pushing and Pulling

When an object is pushed or pulled, the object exerts an **opposing push** or **pull** on whatever is pushing or pulling it.

Pushing

If we push or squeeze a spring, the spring in return exerts its own pushing force on the hands that are squeezing it.

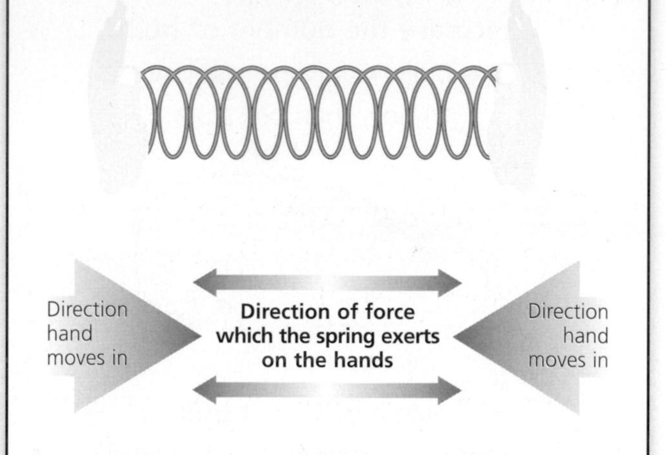

Pulling

If we pull or stretch an elastic band (or spring), the elastic band in return exerts its own pulling force on the hands that are stretching it.

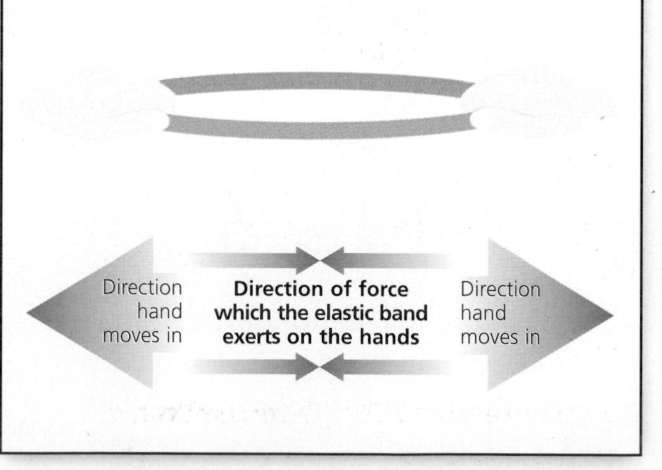

9 Name three forces that act against a moving object.

10 A girl stretches a spring using her hands. Will the spring exert a pushing or a pulling force on her hands? Explain your answer.

Force Due to Gravity

All objects are pulled downwards because of **gravity**. This pull force is called **weight**.

Remember, **weight** and **mass** do not mean the same thing. The mass of an object is the amount of stuff that it contains and is measured in kilograms or grams, whereas force is measured in newtons.

The girl to the right would have the same weight at any point on the Earth's surface. Weight always acts towards the centre of the Earth!

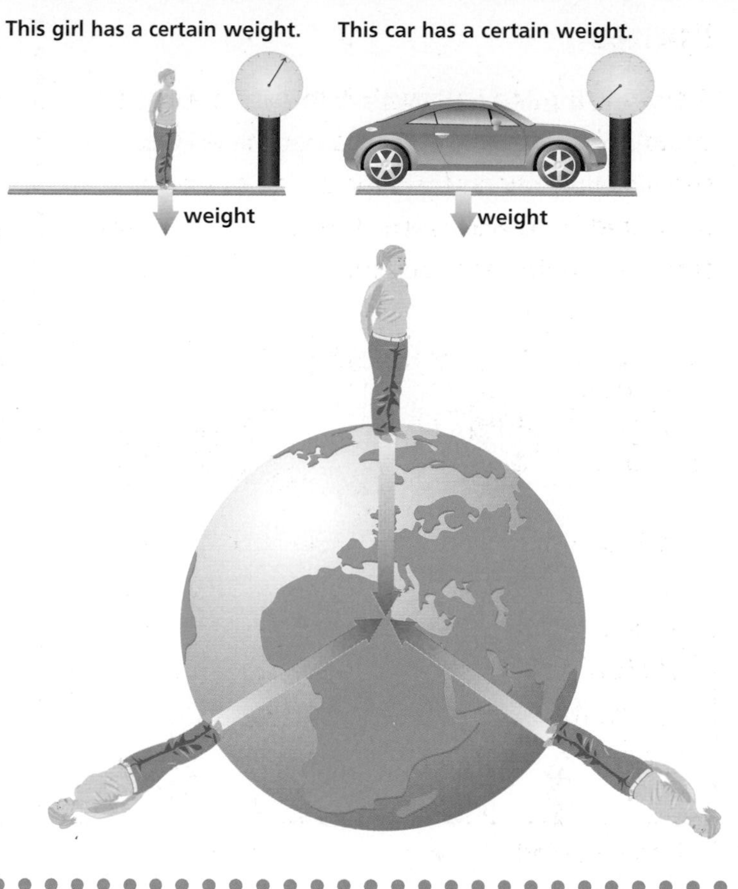

11 What would happen to your weight if you went to the Moon? Why does this happen?

12 What would happen to your weight if you went to Outer Space where there is no gravity?

Measuring Weight

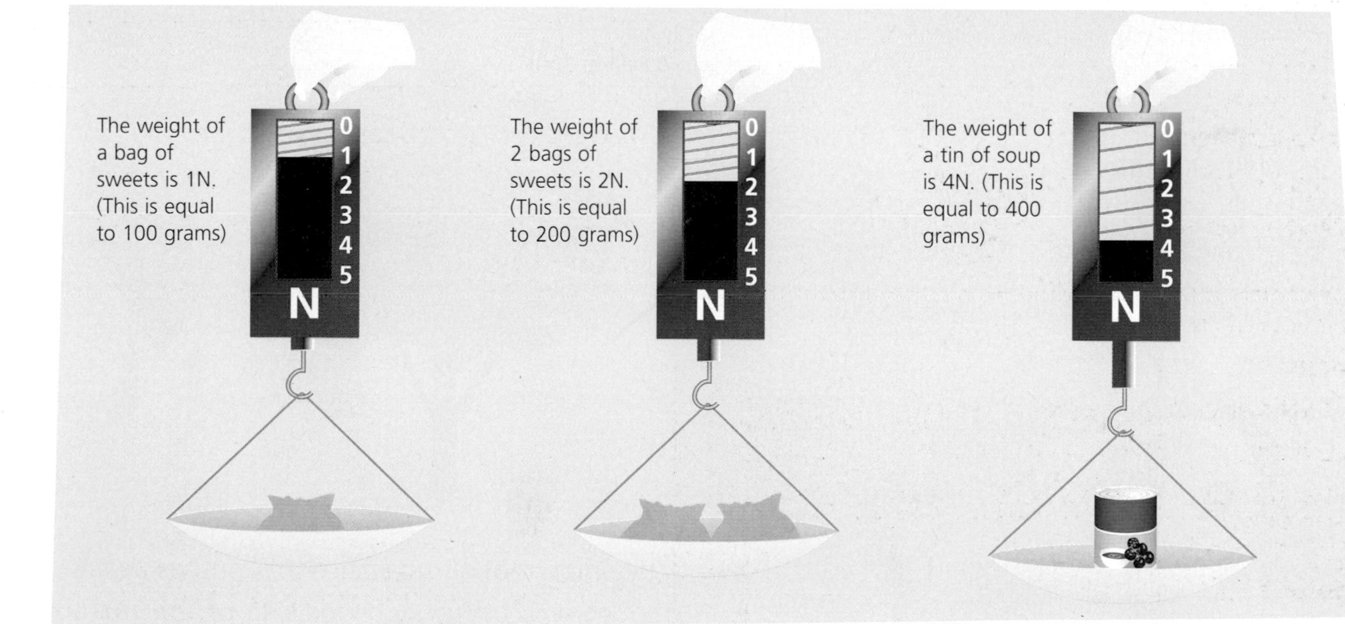

Weight is measured using a **forcemeter**. A forcemeter simply contains a spring which stretches when an object is hung from it.
All forcemeters have a scale on them so that you can 'read off' the weight of the object.

13 What is a forcemeter?

14 Draw a forcemeter showing 3 bags of sweets being weighed.

15 Draw a forcemeter showing a 150 gram bag of sweets being weighed.

Friction

Friction is the force that resists the movement of an object. It always acts in the opposite direction to the direction the object is moving in or attempting to move in. Friction slows moving objects down and it may also prevent an object from starting to move.

A simple way to create friction is to rub your hands together. Friction is created when the two hand surfaces move past each other due to the unevenness between the two surfaces trying to pass over each other. If you were to look at any two surfaces, even the smoothest surfaces, under a microscope they would look rough and uneven. This roughness causes one surface to catch on the other, which creates friction.

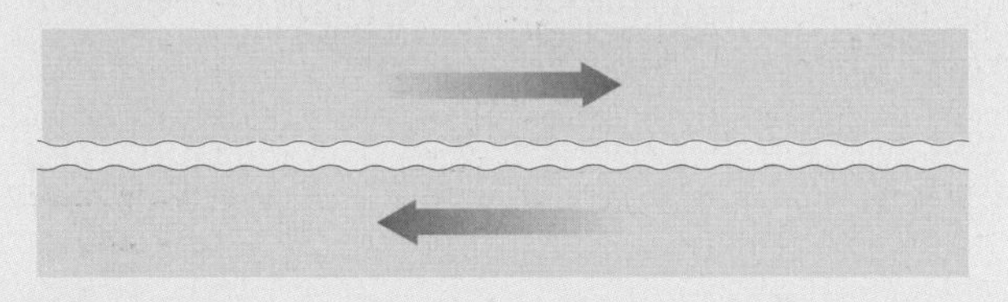

The amount of friction which is created between two surfaces can be large or small:

- A large force of friction is created between the tyres of a bicycle and the road to provide the grip.
- A small force of friction is created between skis and snow to enable the skier to go as fast as possible.

Air Resistance

Air resistance is the force that pushes against a moving object as it passes through the air, slowing the object down.

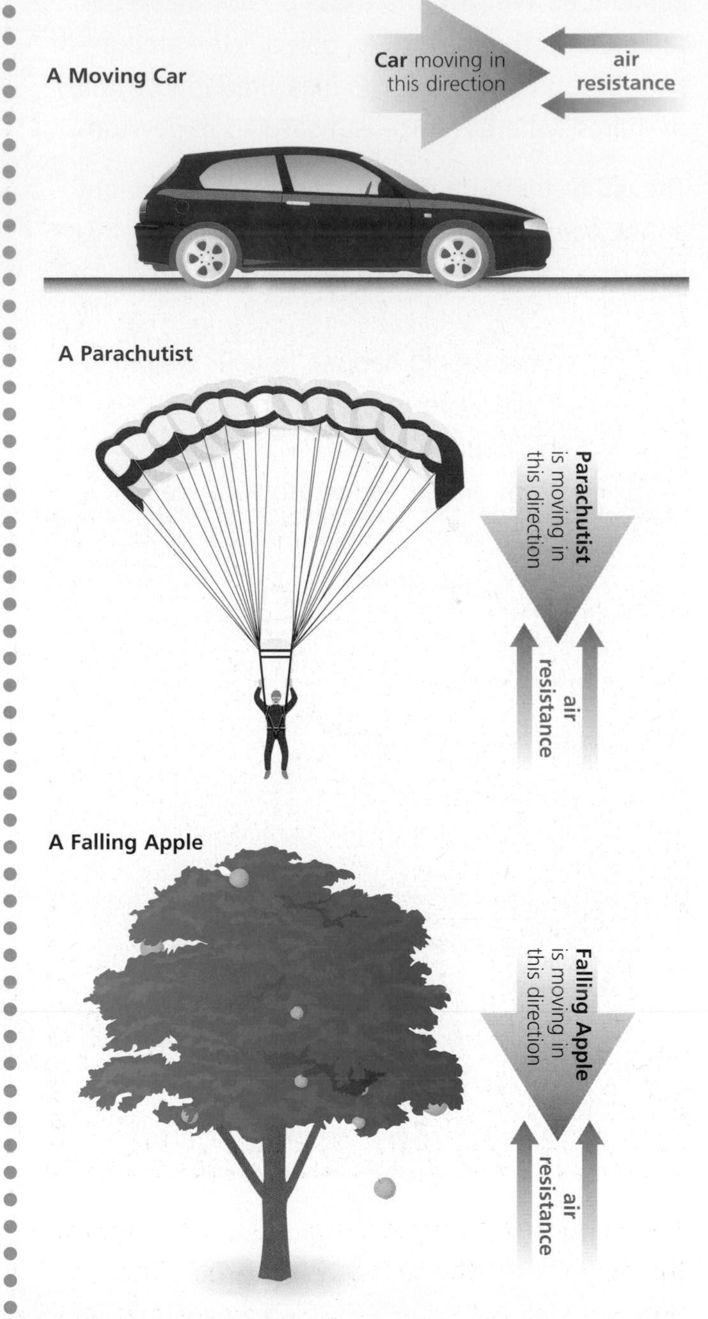

The amount of air resistance that pushes against a moving object depends on the **size of the surface** of the object. A parachute has a very large surface, which means that the parachutist falls much more slowly than the apple, which has a very small surface.

16 Give two other examples where the amount of friction created between two surfaces should ideally be **a)** large **b)** small.

17 Give two other examples where the amount of air resistance would be **a)** large **b)** small.

Water Resistance

Water resistance is the force that pushes against a moving object as it passes through water, slowing the object down.

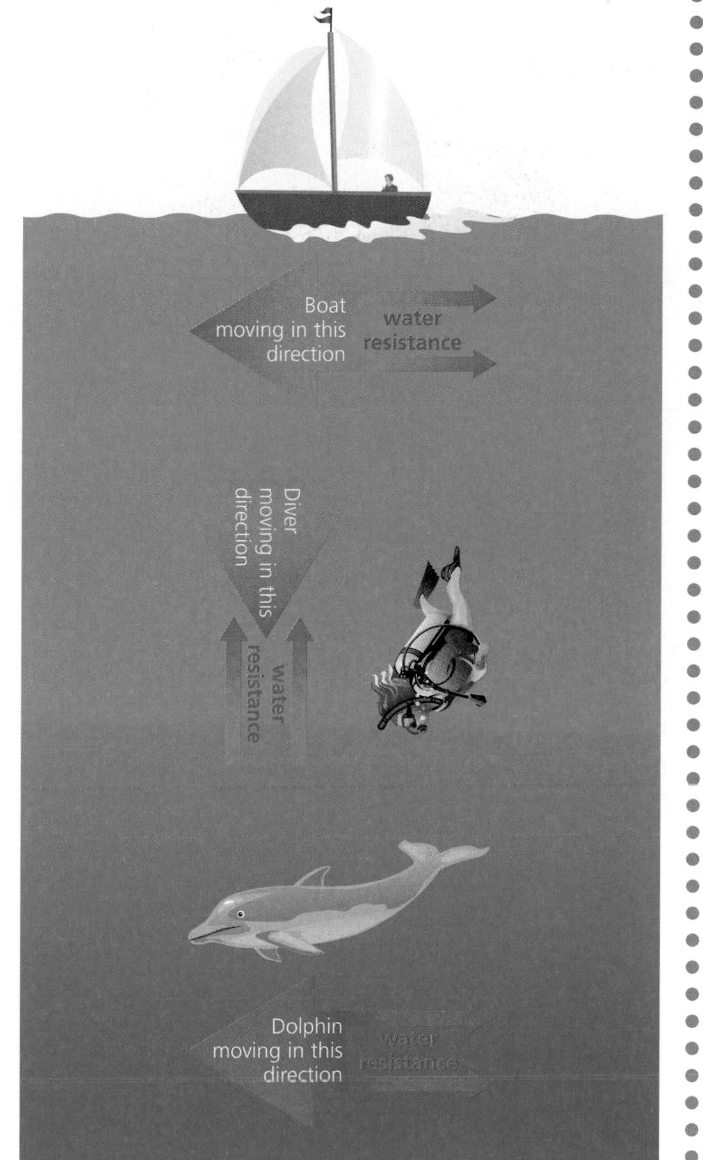

The amount of water resistance that pushes against the dolphin and the sailing boat is small. They are both streamlined in shape, which means that they can 'cut through' the water more easily. The diver is not streamlined (although he can be if he changes his shape) and so the amount of water resistance pushing against him is greater. The diver will 'sink' to the bottom of the sea much more slowly.

18 Give two other examples where the amount of water resistance would be **a)** large **b)** small.

Upthrust

All objects that are put into water experience an **upward force** from the water. This upward force is called **upthrust**. You will have felt this force in action every time you've been in a swimming pool.

A pupil was asked to investigate upthrust. She took an object that sinks in water and first weighed it in air and then when it was put into water. She noticed that the weight of the object goes down when it is put into water. The reason this happens is because the object experiences an upward force, the upthrust, from the water which acts against the weight of the object. This causes the reading on the forcemeter to go down.

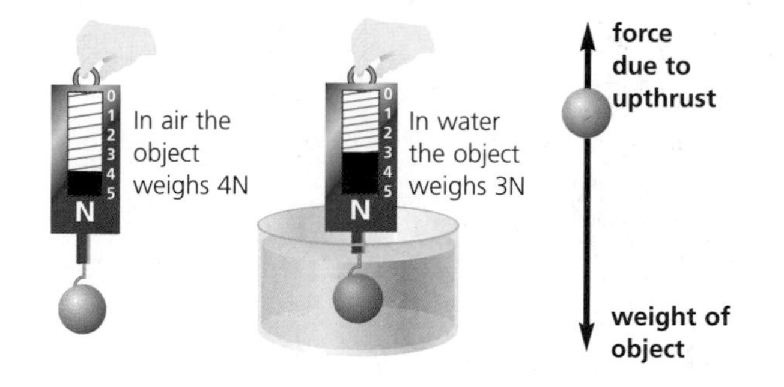

She then took another object that floats. Again she weighed the object in air and then when it was floating on the surface of the water. This time she noticed that the reading on the forcemeter went down to nought. In other words the object weighs nothing! The reason this happens is because the weight of the object acting downwards is **balanced** by the upward force, the upthrust. In other words the forces cancel each other out.

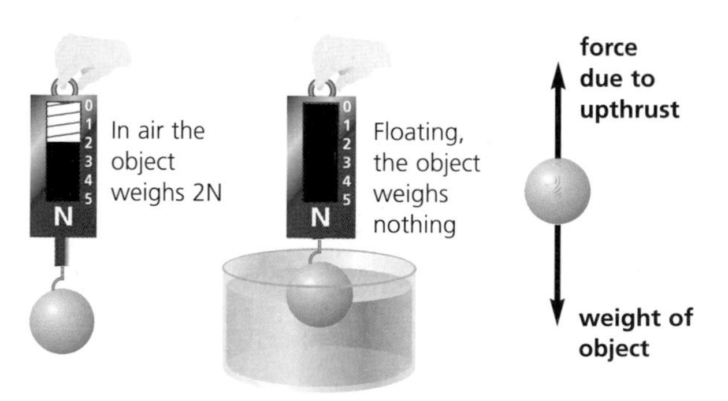

19 An object weighs 10N in the air. If the object floats what is the size of the upthrust?

20 An object weighs 20N in the air. It sinks in water and the reading on the forcemeter is 22N. Can this be correct? Explain your answer.

Magnetic Forces

Magnetism is a weird force. A magnet will only exert a pull force on certain materials, **magnetic materials**. Iron, steel, nickel and cobalt are magnetic materials. All other materials (including every other metal) are **non-magnetic** and a magnet has no effect at all on them.

A magnet can be used to separate iron and aluminium cans when they are being recycled.

The magnet exerts a pull force on the steel cans but...

... has no effect on the aluminium cans...

... or the plastic cups.

21 Sort the following – glass, steel, wood, paper, nickel, iron and gold – into **a)** magnetic materials **b)** non-magnetic materials.

Forces Between Two Magnets

The two ends of a magnet are called **poles**. One end is called the **north (N) pole** and the other end is called the **south (S) pole**.

When the ends of two magnets are brought near each other, two things can happen:

1. **Repulsion** – the two magnets will push each other away (i.e. repel each other) if the ends have the same poles.

2. **Attraction** – the two magnets will pull towards each other (i.e. attract each other) if the ends have different poles.

If we replace one of the magnets with an iron bar (i.e. a magnetic material) the iron bar is attracted towards the south pole and the north pole of the magnet, i.e. it is *always* attracted towards the magnet; there will never be repulsion between a magnetic material and a magnet.

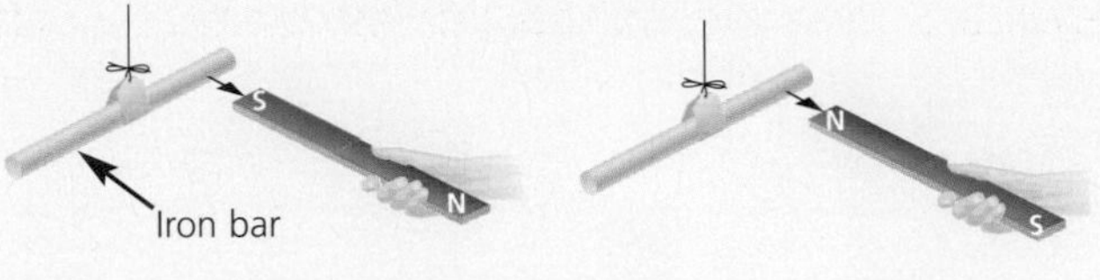

22 Draw a cartoon strip to show how you determine the difference between a magnet and magnetic material.

23 Find out why the two ends of a magnet are called the north pole and the south pole.

Testing the Strength of a Magnet

A simple way to test the strength of a magnet or to compare two or more different magnets is to see how many steel pins each magnet can pick up.

24 Design your own fair test to compare the strength of two different magnets.

Physical Processes

Light

There are many different sources of light. Our main source of light is the Sun. Where there is no light, there is darkness.

The light that travels away from a source is often called a beam or a ray. A beam or ray of light is drawn as a straight line with an arrow on it to show the direction the light is travelling. The further light gets from its source, the more it spreads out.

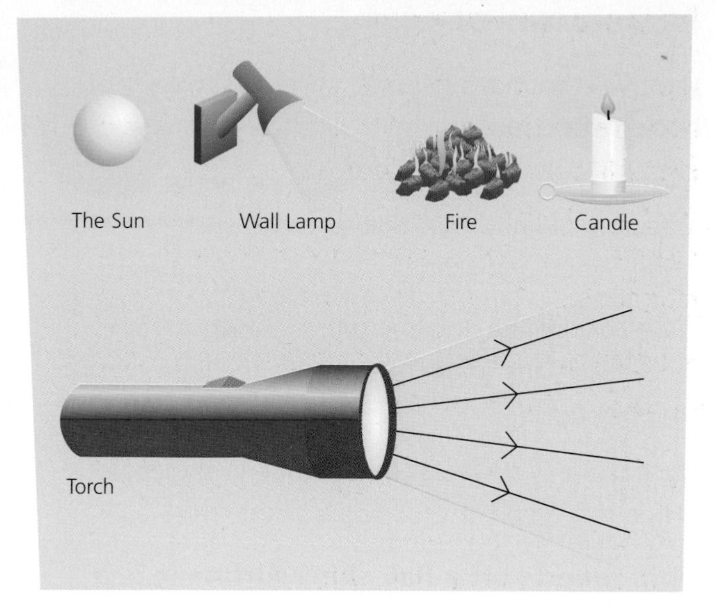

Name 5 other sources of light and draw a diagram of each one.

Shadows

Materials that stop light getting through are called **opaque**. Materials that let light through are called **transparent**. Shadows are formed when the light travelling from a source is blocked by an opaque object.

Because light only travels in a straight line, the shadow cast will always be the same shape as the object that formed it, however, its size can be changed.

Shadows can be made smaller by moving the object further from the light source or moving the screen closer to the object.

26 Draw a diagram showing the shadow formed if the owl is moved closer to the screen.

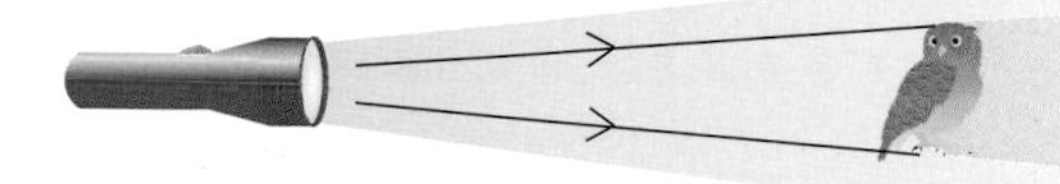

Shadows can be made bigger by:

1 Moving the object nearer the light source.

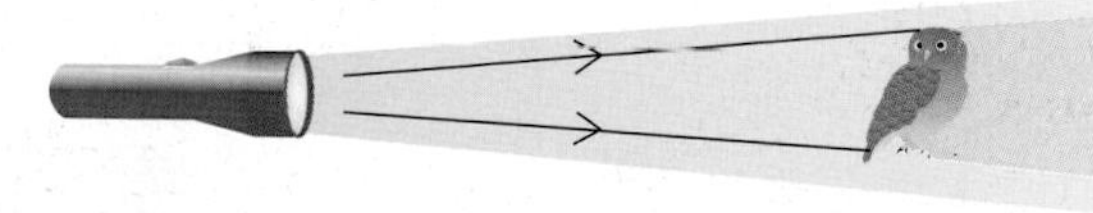

2 Moving the screen further from the object.

Physical Processes

Reflection of Light

Light will 'bounce off' some surfaces. This is called **reflection**.

Mirrors, glass and shiny surfaces are better reflectors of light than dull surfaces, such as stone, wood and fabric.

If we change the angle at which the light hits the surface, the angle of the reflected light changes too.

For flat, shiny surfaces, this change in the angle of the reflected light follows a simple rule:

Light reflects off a flat, shiny surface (e.g. a mirror) at exactly the same angle that it hits it (see diagrams opposite).

The reflection of light by a mirror can be very useful. A **periscope** uses two mirrors to reflect light (see diagram alongside). Light reflects off one mirror onto another mirror, enabling us to see objects over a high barrier, e.g. a wall.

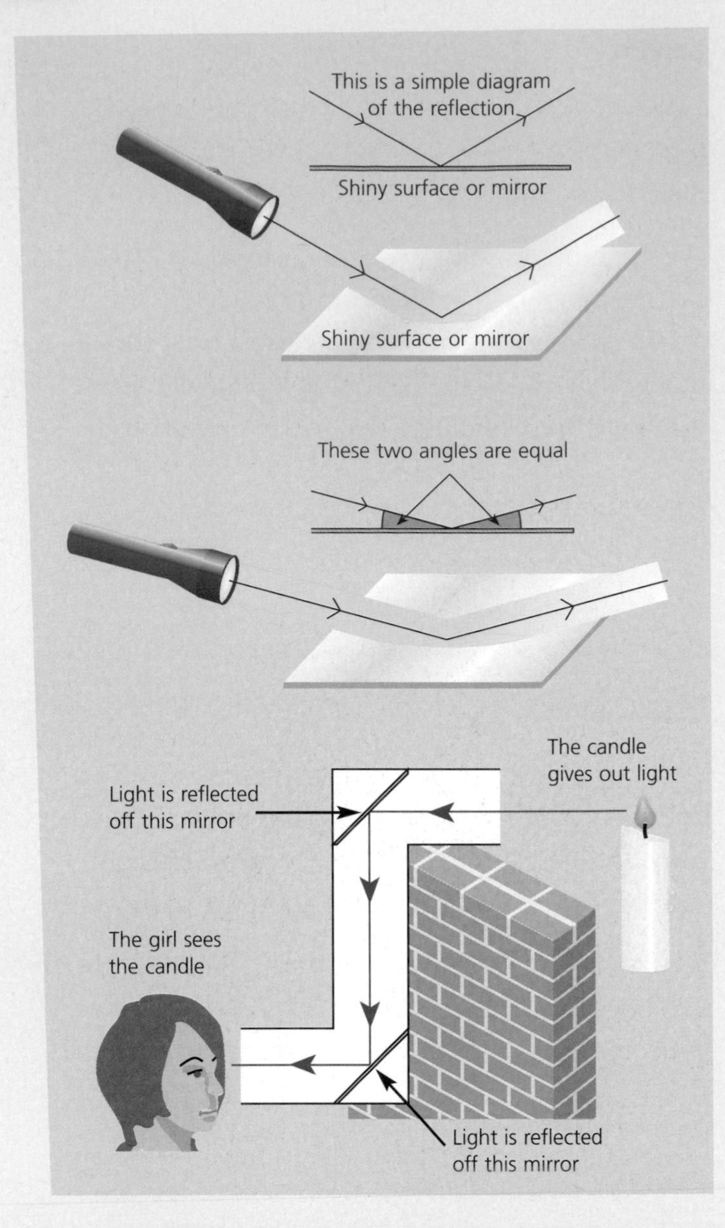

27 **a)** Name three good reflectors of light.
b) Name three bad reflectors of light.

28 Find three other devices that have mirrors in them.

How We See Things

We can see light sources because the light they give out enters our eyes. We can see other objects, e.g. this page, people around us, because light from a light source is reflected off them into our eyes. If a mirror reflects the light from an object into our eyes then we will see the object. If we close our eyes we cannot see the things around us because our eyelids block out the light.

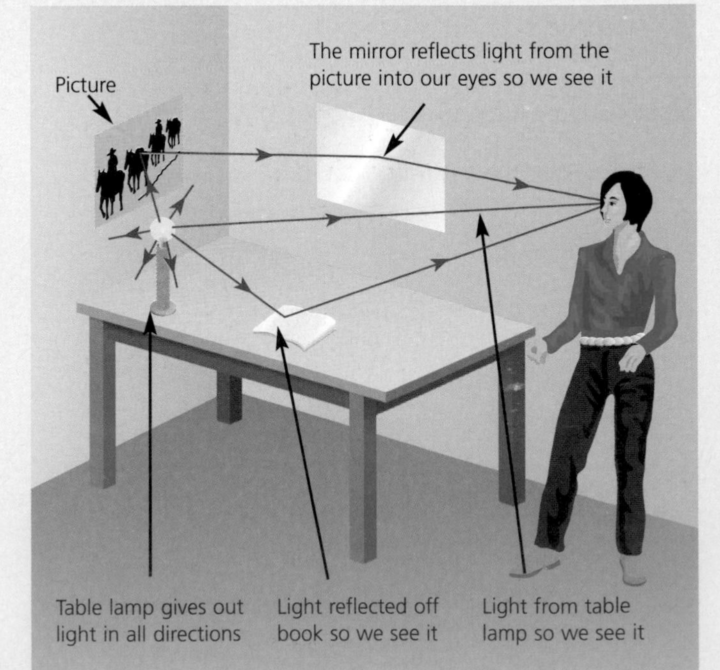

29 How is it possible for you to see your teacher at school?

30 Would you be able to see your teacher if the classroom suddenly went completely dark. Explain your answer.

Sound

Sound is produced when an object or a material is made to move forwards and backwards quickly. We say that the object or material is **vibrating**. Most of the time we can't see the object or material vibrating since the vibrations are too fast and too small.

Some vibrations are visible however, e.g. if you pluck one of the strings on a guitar you can see the string vibrating, although you can't see an individual vibration.

When tapped, a tuning fork vibrates too fast for us to see. If the tapped tuning fork just touches the water, the vibration causes ripples and splashes.

When hit, a drumskin vibrates, again too fast for us to see. If small pieces of paper are placed on the drum, the vibration causes them to jump up and down.

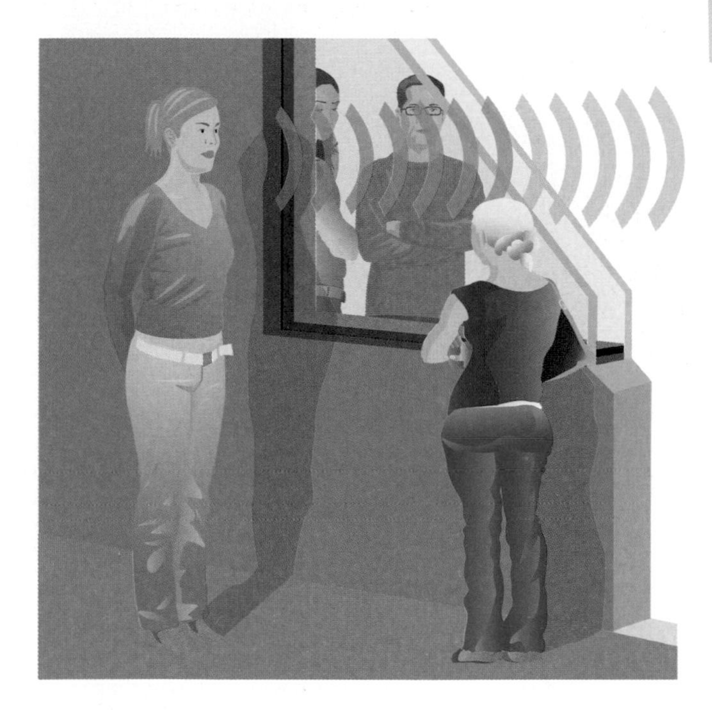

We hear the sound produced by an object because these vibrations travel from the object to our ears. Sound can travel through many different materials. You can hear a sound produced outside your classroom. This sound will travel through air, stone, brick, glass, wood and many other materials to reach your ears.

31 Draw diagrams of three other objects that produce sound.

32 What part of your body vibrates when you produce sound?

Stopping Sound

Too much sound reaching your ears can be a problem, as it can damage your hearing. People who work in noisy places often wear ear muffs or ear plugs to muffle some of the sound reaching their ears.

Soft materials, such as carpets and curtains, are very good at muffling sound to stop it travelling any further. Hard materials such as stone and metal are not very good at muffling sound and they help the sound to travel further.

33 Why is it important to reduce the amount of noise reaching your ears?

34 Name 5 materials that are **a)** good at muffling sound **b)** bad at muffling sound.

Physical Processes

The sound made by a vibrating object or material can be changed in two ways:

1 **Pitch** – the pitch of a sound is a measure of how 'high' or how 'low' it is. You can investigate pitch by doing a simple experiment, in which a ruler is clamped to the end of a table:

If you pluck the ruler you will hear a sound of a certain pitch.

With a shorter length of ruler, you will hear a sound of a higher pitch.

With a longer length of ruler, you will hear a sound of a lower pitch.

Young girls usually talk with a high pitch

Men usually talk with a low pitch

2 **Loudness** – the loudness of a sound is a measure of how loud or how quiet it is. Yet again you can investigate loudness by doing a simple experiment, again with a ruler clamped to the end of a table:

If you pluck the ruler you will hear a sound of a certain loudness.

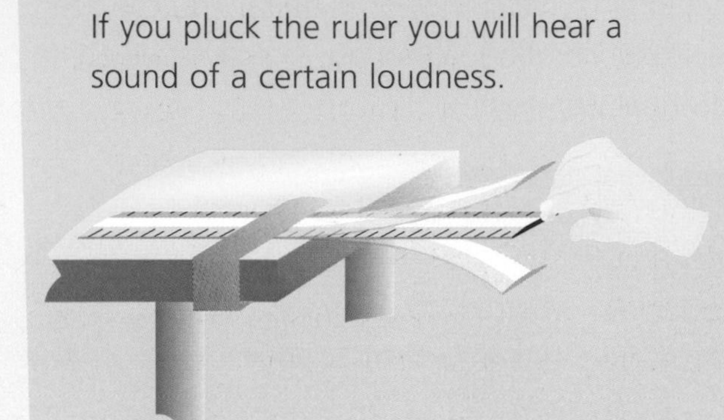

If you pluck the ruler harder you will hear a louder sound.

If you pluck the ruler more gently you will hear a quieter sound.

35 What would you have to do to the ruler if you wanted a sound that is:

a) high pitch and loud?

b) low pitch and quiet?

c) high pitch and quiet?

Stringed Instruments

Stringed instruments make a sound when their strings are plucked and made to **vibrate**. A guitar is a simple stringed musical instrument.

There are three ways that the pitch of the sound produced by a guitar string can be changed:

1. Thinner strings of the same length and tightness are higher pitched. Most guitars have six strings of different thicknesses.
2. Shorter strings of the same thickness and tightness are higher pitched. By pressing the string onto the frets on the guitar neck, the length of a string can be altered.
3. Tighter strings of the same length and thickness are higher pitched. The guitar has tuning keys to alter the tightness.

There is one way that the loudness of the sound produced by a guitar string can be changed – by plucking the string harder. The harder you pluck, the louder the sound.

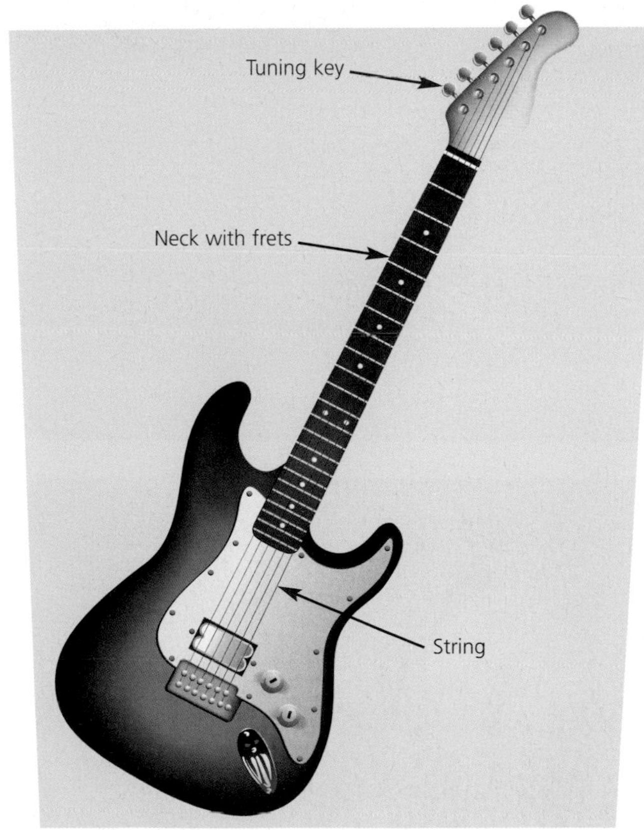

36 Describe how you would produce a high pitched, quiet sound on a guitar.

Wind Instruments

Wind instruments make a sound because the air inside the instrument is made to vibrate. If you blow across the top of a bottle with some water in it, the air inside the bottle vibrates and a sound is heard. The pitch of the sound depends on the amount of water in the bottle.

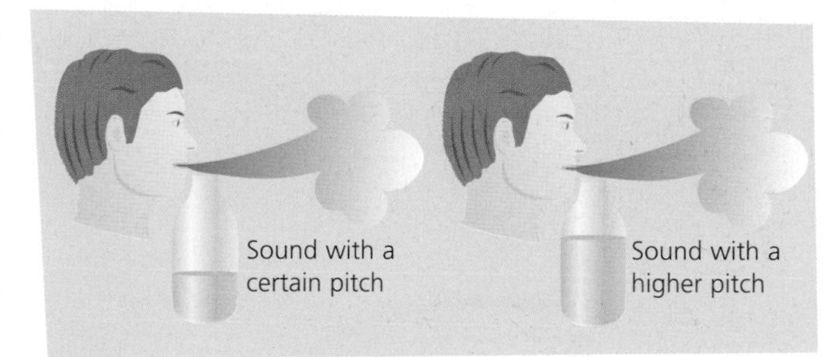

One wind instrument that allows you to play sounds of different pitches is the recorder. The pitch is changed by placing your fingers on one or more of the holes. This changes the length of air which is vibrating inside the recorder. The loudness is changed by blowing harder or softer.

37 Find out about another two wind instruments and how they produce sounds of different pitches.

A Drum

The loudness of a drum depends on how hard you hit it.

The pitch of a drum depends on the...

1. **tightness of the drum skin** – a tighter skin is higher pitched. (The tightness of the drum skin can be changed by using the screws on the side of the drum.)
2. **size of the drum** – a small drum is higher pitched.

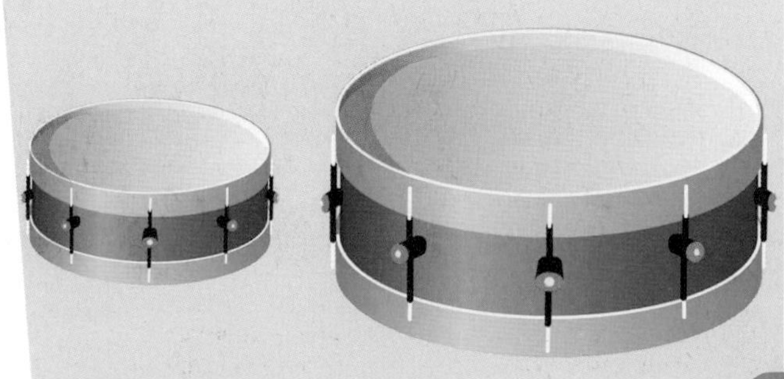

Physical Processes

Sun, Earth and Moon

The **Earth** on which we live is constantly moving around the Sun. The direction the Earth moves in is called an **orbit**. It takes the Earth just over 365 days to orbit the Sun once. This is **one year**.

At the same time as the Earth is orbiting the Sun, the Moon is in orbit around the Earth. It takes the Moon 28 days to orbit the Earth once. We know it takes 28 days because of the way its appearance changes during a 28 day period. After 28 days the Moon looks exactly like it was 28 days previously! In between, the Moon has many 'new faces'.

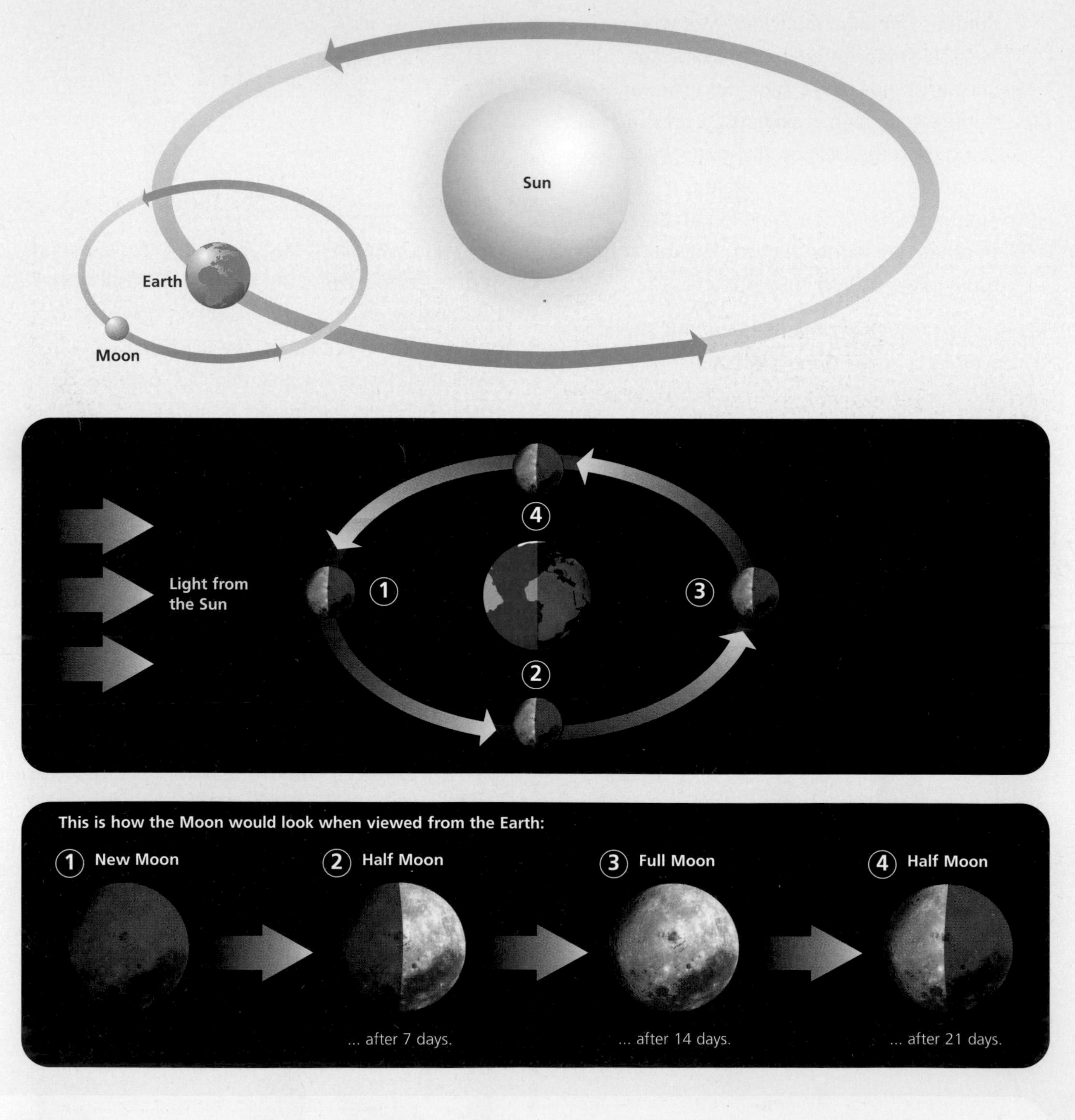

38 Draw a diagram of the Sun, the Earth and the Moon showing their orbits.

39 Draw diagrams to show the appearance of the Moon after 4 days, 11 days, 18 days, and 25 days.

Shape of the Sun, Earth and Moon

The Sun, Earth and Moon are all approximately shaped like a ball. They are **spherical** in shape.

A very long time ago people thought that the Earth was flat! If you look at a boat that sails out to sea, you will notice that as the boat goes further and further away it starts to disappear. This happens because the surface of the Earth is curved. In other words the Earth is spherical.

In the last 40 years spectacular pictures have been taken of the Earth from Space. These pictures provide further proof that the Earth is spherical.

40 Which part of a ship would you see first as it sailed towards you from over the horizon?

Size of the Sun, Earth and Moon

The diagram on page 48 gives the impression that the Sun is a bit bigger than the Earth, and the Earth is a bit bigger than the Moon. This is not the case.

If the Sun was the size of a beachball, then...

- the Earth would be about the size of a small pea
- the Moon would be about the size of a small bead.

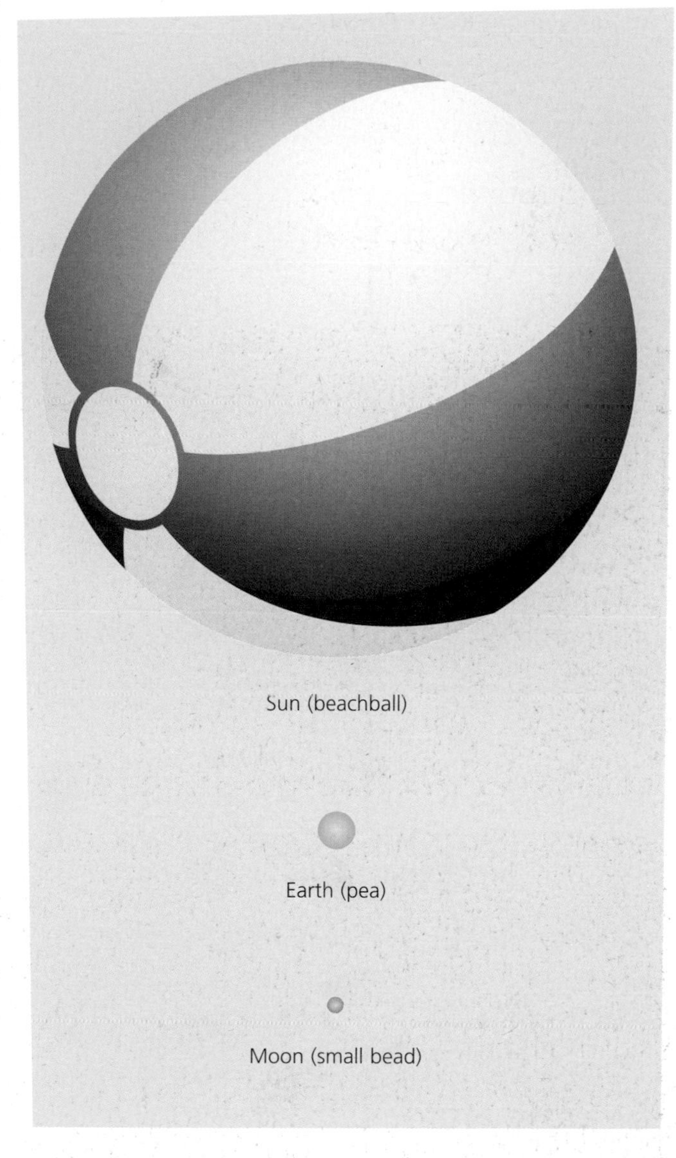

Draw a poster showing the Sun, the Earth and the Moon and their approximate sizes.

Physical Processes

The Earth

As we have seen, the Earth is constantly moving around the Sun. As the Earth moves it is also spinning around, just like a spinning top, on its **axis**.

The Earth completes one spin, or **rotation**, every **24 hours** giving us daytime (for the part of the Earth which is facing the Sun) and night-time (for the part of the Earth which is facing away from the Sun).

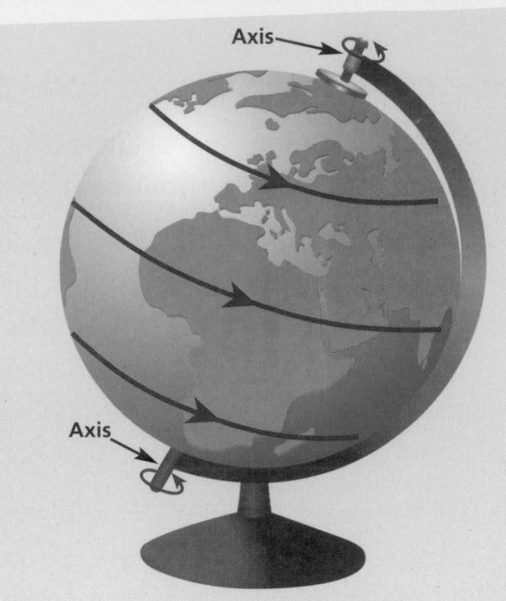

The idea of the rotation of the Earth can be seen using a globe.

42 Name 5 countries where it is night-time when it is just beginning to get dark in Britain (you can use a globe to help you).

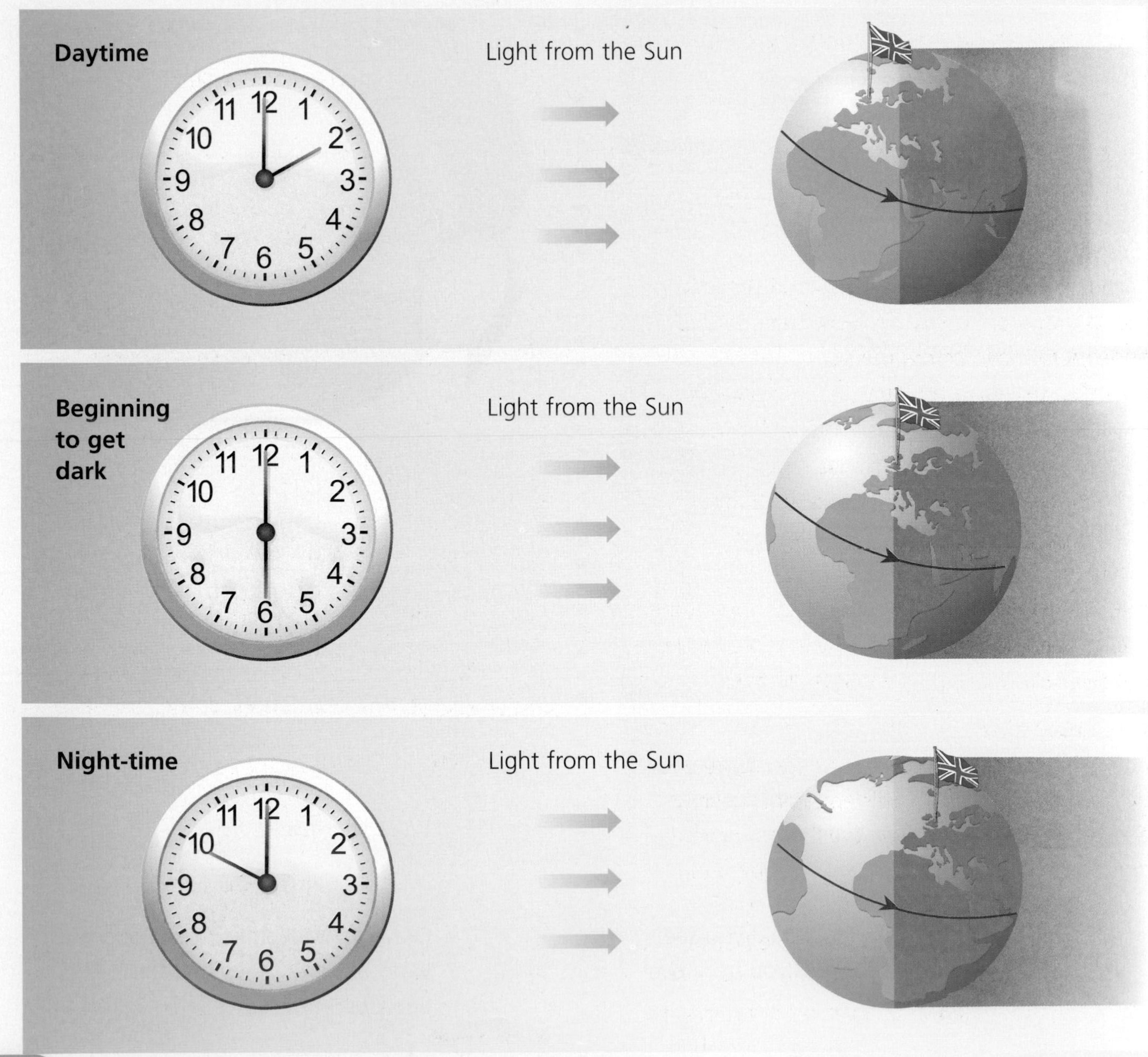

The Changing Position of the Sun

Every day the Sun rises or appears in the sky in an easterly direction. This is called sunrise.

Throughout the day the Sun then appears to move across the sky following a curved path. It is at its highest position at midday.

Later on the Sun sets or disappears from the sky in a westerly direction. This is called sunset.

A compass can be used to check the direction in which the Sun rises and sets.

Record the sunrise and sunset times for a week. Are they all the same?

Length of Shadow Produced by the Sun

Throughout the day the **length** and **direction** of the shadow formed by the Sun changes as the Sun appears to move across the sky:

- **In the morning** the Sun is low in the sky and in an easterly direction. The shadow formed is **long** and points towards the **west**.
- **At midday** when the Sun is at its highest, the shadow formed is at its **shortest** and points towards the **north**.
- **In the afternoon** the Sun is again low in the sky and in a westerly direction. The shadow formed is again **long** and points towards the **east**.

One Last Point:

As we have said, the Sun appears to move across the sky during the day. This apparent movement of the Sun is created because the Earth is spinning around on its axis. The Sun isn't moving at all!

44 Draw diagrams to show the house and its shadow at **a)** 10 o'clock in the morning **b)** 2 o'clock in the afternoon.

Notes

These pages have been provided so that pupils can write in the answers to some of the questions set in the book.

Notes

These pages have been provided so that pupils can write in the answers to some of the questions set in the book.

Notes

These pages have been provided so that pupils can write in the answers to some of the questions set in the book.

Acknowledgements

The author and publisher would like to thank everyone who has contributed to this book.

p.6 ©iStockphoto.com / Fanelie Rosier
p.6 ©iStockphoto.com / Jami Garrison
p.10 ©iStockphoto.com / Joshua Blake
p.11 ©iStockphoto.com / Paul IJsendoorn
p.18 ©iStockphoto.com / Gennadij Kurilin
p.27 ©iStockphoto.com / Paul IJsendoorn
p.34 ©iStockphoto.com / Brandon Laufenberg
p.34 ©iStockphoto.com / kim bryant
p.34 ©iStockphoto.com / Peter Finnie
p.47 ©iStockphoto.com / Joe Lera
p.50 ©iStockphoto.com / Russell Tate

Every effort has been made to contact the holders of copyright material, but if any have been inadvertently overlooked, the publisher will be pleased to make the necessary arrangements at the first opportunity.

ISBN: 978-1-903068-36-6

Published by Letts and Lonsdale

Editor: Grace A. Adams

Cover and concept design: Sarah Duxbury

Designer: Sarah Duxbury

Artwork: Lonsdale and HL Studios

Letts and Lonsdale make every effort to ensure that all paper used in our books is made from wood pulp obtained from sustainable and well-managed forests.

Index